#45-95 BK Bud May 95

NORTH CAROLINA
STATE BOARD OF COMMUNITY COLLEGES
LIBRARIES
SOUTHEASTERN COMMUNITY COLLEGE

P9-CCR-757

SOUTHEASTERN COMMUNITY
COLLEGE LIBRARY
WHITEVILLE, NC 28472

HV
41.9
.U5
D69
1993

Fund Raising 101

How to Raise Money
for Charities

William L. "Bill" Doyle

SOUTHEASTERN COMMUNITY
COLLEGE LIBRARY
WHITEVILLE, NC 28472

American Fund Raising Institute
Publishing Division
United States of America

i

American Fund Raising Institute® recognizes the importance of preserving good books. Therefore, it is our policy to have these books published in the United States and printed on acid-free paper.

Copyright © 1993 by:
    American Fund Raising Institute®
    Publishing Division
    United States of America

All rights reserved. Any part of this work beyond that permitted by Section 107 or 108 of the 1976 United States Copyright Act without permission of the Publisher is illegal.

Library of Congress Cataloging-in-Publication Data:

Doyle, William L. "Bill"., 1941-
    Fund Raising 101 : how to raise money for charities
  / William L. "Bill" Doyle
        ISBN 0-9639846-0-8 (cloth)
        1. Fund Raising. 2. Title 3. Doyle, William L "Bill"

                Library of Congress Catalog Card Number:
                            93-091058

                International Standard Book Number:
                            0-9639846-0-8

Copyedited by Shirley Covington
Jacket Design by Myra Danehy
Special Effort by June Childress
Printed in Kingsport, Tennessee by Arcata Graphics

First Edition

DEDICATION

To my wife, Toni, and our family.

I love you and thank you for your patience
and understanding
as I immersed myself in this project.

To the employees, the physicians, and especially my staff and the volunteers of Holston Valley Hospital, Kingsport, Tennessee. They know the meaning of Philanthropy—The Love of Mankind.

And

To the many charities that I've had the pleasure of working with, hospitals, colleges, human services such as Boys and Girls Clubs, Ys, Boy and Girl Scouts, and Junior Achievement. And also agencies such as the March of Dimes, Lung Association, Heart, Cancer, Lupus, and sight, as well as a bar association, animal shelters, public TV and radio, various United Ways, various political campaigns, and many denominations of worship.

34.50

Preface

Any book, lecture, or conversation concerning where to begin in fund raising is likely to start with discussions around the premise that reminds us there are three sectors in American society: business, government, and ours, referred to by many names, such as the third sector, the private sector, or the voluntary sector.

There are three characteristics of the third sector that make it unique. The first is that the organizations that comprise the sector are private, governed by a board of volunteers, and intended to serve all citizens equally. Second, the sector is growing at an unbelievable rate; in 1992 the combined income of over 1.3 million tax exempt organizations exceeded $124 billion. If you add the estimated value of volunteer time at nearly $150 billion dollars, you have a fair piece of the GNP. And third, the third sector is important to the American way of life. Millions volunteer their time and money and millions more depend on the benefits provided, such as medical care, education, drug treatment, AIDS treatment, and so on.

It is well known that most modern movements began in the voluntary sector. Examples include: civil rights, the women's movement, and dealing with environmental problems.

Because of this tremendous growth, Fund Raising 101 was written expressly for the beginning fund raiser, professional or volunteer. There are many very good books that address the needs of seasoned professionals, but this is the first for the newcomer. I firmly believe that it should be required reading for everyone just starting out in the field.

Managing a not-for-profit has never been easy, but with so many more charities it is even harder today. The critical challenge is for volunteer boards and staff to use their various skills together as an effective team to increase revenue, lower costs, and most significant, accomplish their mission.

This book deals with all aspects of fund raising. To start with, it assumes that any well organized and successful development program will have competent, knowledgeable, hard working staff, with sincere, dedicated, generous, and supportive volunteers. And most important, it tells you what you need to know in a logical order.

There are nineteen chapters, beginning with the basic needs for both staff and volunteers. You might say that you will learn what you need to know in chapters 1 through 8 before you begin the actual fund process in chapters 9 through 16. The final three chapters, 17, 18, and 19 deal with proposal writing, evaluating your fund raising process, and a brief look at Total Quality Management.

One of the joys in writing this book is being able to relate some of the things I've learned in such a way as to be helpful to people just starting out in the fund raising profession. I have had many opportunities to work with small charities, helping with training, organization, and project activation. I've experienced the thrill of seeing ideas turn into dollars. And, I have received enormous gratification from knowing that there are real people who benefit from the increased dollars. And finally, I've made many lasting friends.

Remember, everything in this book is deliberately written to be helpful to the beginning and intermediate fund raiser and their volunteers. Advanced fund raisers will find that each chapter is expressed simply, without the cumbersome details that often bog us down. Frankly, after each chapter I have asked myself, why did I ever get away from doing it this way? We all know that keeping it simple is often the best way.

Whether you are a beginner or an old pro, I hope you find Fund Raising 101 helpful in your fund raising life.

Bill

TABLE OF CONTENTS

Part One

Chapter One

The Role of Staff

No one has more effect on the fund-raising process than the motivated, knowledgeable, full-time staff person. That is why I begin this book by describing the role and responsibilities of the development officer. The points covered apply to all the professional development staff who work for a fund-raising organization.

The role and responsibilities of the development officer begin with a deep personal commitment to the institution's cause. Without this depth of commitment, the staff might just as well be working for any organization. A major hazard of the job is the many hours that committed development officers put in. They invariably come in to the office early and stay late. They often work on the weekends and at nights. It's not hard to understand why so many burn out.

A development professional should have many skills, but the ability to manage volunteers is the most crucial. It is considered by many senior development officers to be the most important asset.

Managing Volunteers

Volunteers come in all shapes and sizes, from all walks of life, and from all strata of society. The professional fund raiser's greatest challenge has been, and will always be, to organize and manage the volunteer corps effectively.

Most management axioms recommend that for peak efficiency, managers should manage no more than five direct reports

1

(people). Yet, in five short years, our small eight-person office of three professionals, one assistant, two secretaries, a data manager, and a bookkeeper has gone from managing the activities of less than 100 volunteers to managing those of 1,500. At least once a year, another 5,000 volunteers participate in a project that benefits our institution.

How can we do this effectively? We can't pay the volunteers. They can't be fired. They aren't promoted or demoted, given raises, or anything else. The truth is that, there isn't one single method of managing volunteers that works effectively. There are hundreds! Understanding this fact is a vital first step in working with these people.

A good first step in managing volunteers effectively is to learn what each one is interested in and what they want to do with their voluntary time. Once you have this information you are able to determine how to direct their energies more effectively. How can you attain this information? You can interview new volunteers, asking about their interests, likes and dislikes, to determine their potential strengths and weaknesses in the fund-raising arena. They will usually tell you *how* they want to be managed.

To the volunteer, the interview should come across as a casual conversation. In reality, I'm gathering facts, about personality traits, volunteer leadership experience, fund-raising knowledge, and the like. An example of a question that might be posed to a volunteer seeking involvement in a project is, "Yes, John, I am interested in expanding our animal shelter. How would you suggest we go about doing it?"

Once you have that information, here's where the management comes in. "Okay, John, what part are you willing to be responsible for? Will you be willing to take direction from me? If so, how far do you want me to go in holding your feet to the fire?"

The personalities found among volunteers is as varied as the number of people represented. The good development officer is constantly managing strong personalities, weak personalities, and all degrees in between. In addition, volunteers' motivations differ

The Role of Staff

widely and can affect your management style. Motivations can include returning a favor, personal ego, résumé building, upbringing, commitment to the community, business contacts, a desire to see the charity succeed, altruism, and many, many more.

Other Responsibilities

Other responsibilities of the development professional include knowledge and talent in the fund-raising profession, as well as willingness to provide leadership by example. The professional must have integrity, confidence, a positive attitude, honesty, and fair-mindedness.

A job description for a development officer includes six major functions:
1. Knowledge and understanding of fund-raising techniques.
2. Loyal support of the volunteer leadership.
3. Careful management of the day-to-day operation of the office within the guidelines established by the volunteer board.
4. Providing the link between the board and the institution, government agencies, and development staff.
5. Serving as the external spokesperson for the institution.
6. Providing stability and continuity over the long run.

Other responsibilities of a development officer include research as it applies to finding volunteers and donor prospects and getting pertinent information about each.

The development officer also assumes the responsibility of developing most first drafts of any written fund-raising material that is produced. This usually includes the drafting of the by-laws, the annual plan, the five-year plan, policies concerning the acceptance of gifts, appeal letters, and so on.

Details can make or break any not-for-profit organization. The staff must be responsible for the seemingly minor---but very important---details. An example is making sure that "thank-you" letters go out to donors in a timely manner. Prospective gift makers must be researched properly, and proposals for financial support must include the correct materials. A call on a very good prospect for a major gift can be lost simply because of the misspelling of the prospect's name. Be prudent and thorough, and you have a good chance of reaping a bountiful harvest.

Successful development professionals know that persistence and follow-up on a prospect is often the key to getting the gift. Convincing volunteers of the importance of persistence is an important duty of the development professional. Many times I have seen the weak at heart let a significant gift slip through their fingers because they didn't want to face the prospect again. It's the development officer's obligation to inspire and encourage the volunteers to "hang in there" until the donor gives a definitive answer.

Persistence

It's up to the professional to determine how to finesse the exact and correct amount of persistence. Just a dab too much can cause a "no" or, even worse, a "go to blazes." Special skills in the art of reading people, along with patience and practice, are needed.

One of the funnier stories I've heard having to do with persistence involves a tremendous volunteer, Mr. James Haslam II, President and CEO of the Pilot Oil Corporation in Knoxville, Tennessee, who was the guest speaker at a major donor appreciation dinner when he told this story. It seems that when he was a young man just beginning to have some success with his company, one of Knoxville's major not-for-profits was entering into a capital campaign. Like many people, Jim had agreed to make five calls. Back in those days, according to Jim, you got only one prospect card at a time. You didn't move on to the second prospect until you had completed the first. For reasons he didn't remember, Jim had been assigned the card of a rich old miser who was famous for chewing up and spitting out young fellows like him. The old man was evaluated at $50,000, and Jim had no hope of getting anything. Marshalling his courage, Jim reluctantly made the call. He patiently described the charity's case and wove a very compelling

The Role of Staff

story in support of it. Much to his surprise, the old gentleman thanked Jim and indicated he was going to write him a check for a $1,000.

Jim was delighted and he found himself whistling as he steered his automobile in the direction of the campaign consultant's office. His description of the consultant was typical of many I have met from that period. The consultant was a sullen old codger, rather short and stocky. He always had a disgusting cigar butt in his mouth that looked as if he might have picked it up after someone else had thrown it away. He never removed his beat-up, sweat-stained, brown felt hat that was also typical of the period. His manner was gruff and comparable to that of a person who had a red-hot poker under his arm. Suffice it to say, this burly old man had struck the fear of God into the hearts of many who were just trying to do their civic duty.

When Jim arrived at the consultant's office, he bounded up the steps, floated into his office, and placed the pledge card on the consultant's desk. The consultant slowly picked up the card. Pinching it between a pudgy thumb and forefinger, he held up the card to Jim and said in a deep, raspy voice, "Take this back and tell him if it's the best he can do, we don't need it."

Jim's heart sank. Dejected and wondering how on earth he was going to find the words to explain this to the miser, he drove around for over an hour. Finally, after mustering up sufficient courage and working out his speech, he called again on the prospect. The second call was a great learning experience for Jim, he managed to raise the miser up to $25,000. It wasn't $50,000, but the consultant took it with a grunt and gave him another card.

The point of this story is to reinforce the importance of persistence. Since that first experience, Jim has no doubt upgraded many low gifts that would have otherwise been lost to the charity in need.

It's our responsibility to teach persistence to our volunteers as the need arises.

Fund Raising 101

Evaluation

That brings us to the responsibility of evaluation. When done immediately following the completion of a project, a thorough evaluation of the revenue, expenses, manpower, timing, and all other pertinent data should provide many answers that you will need when deciding whether or not the project merits repeating next year.

A few years ago, I was consulting with a charity that engaged me to advise them on how to improve their revenue. Each year, they conducted two fund-raising projects that required enormous manpower and other resources. When I asked how successful they were with these two projects, the answer was, "We don't make a lot of money, but we make a lot of friends. We want you to show us what project to conduct that makes money."

Almost any project that your charity conducts, unless other goals are agreed on in advance, should do the following three things.

1. Make friends.
2. Raise money.
3. Provide education to the community about your charity.

You and your volunteers are just kidding yourselves if you spend some of your financial resources, use up a good portion of your volunteer manpower, and wind up with less money than when you started. Don't let this happen to your organization.

Stability and Continuity

All the development officer's responsibilities are important, but the one that is the most difficult for volunteers to understand is stability and continuity in the organization's staff. Nothing is harder on any charity than constant or frequent turnover of staff. Volunteers and donors alike will lose confidence in any charity that cannot or will not lock in on a permanent professionally trained staff. Yet, I see turnover where it doesn't need to be.

A friend who was newly employed by the board of a small college was surprised to learn that the average tenure in his position

6

had been twenty-three months. It's not hard for me to understand why. His volunteers insisted that they knew more about running his organization than he did. Due to human nature, this problem will always present a challenge. As a result, he stayed only seven months.

I have observed that being a fund-raising executive has at least one similarity to being the pastor of a church. These two positions need the support and help of their volunteers, but it seems to be human nature for the volunteers or the church members to complain about these leaders. This seems illogical. My friend had a staff of seven who needed his strong leadership, as did the many committees that wanted and needed immediate answers. For reasons I'll never understand, they drive one executive director after another away.

The senior development officer, regardless of title, should have the authority to hire, train, discipline, and fire his direct reports, without having permission to do so by volunteer boards. This assignment of authority to the senior development officer is borne out by the leading authors of not-for-profit management books.

As in any business, managers are not perfect. Yet, it often seems that not-for-profit boards want and expect a higher degree of perfection in charity management than they would
expect of themselves or anyone else in the business world and government.

Another responsibility of the development officer is to act as a bridge, or conduit, between the volunteers and the charity being served. Sometimes, in the smaller charities where the staff may be wearing a dozen hats, communication is not a problem, for the charity is being managed by the same staff person who is raising the funds and mopping the floors.

In larger not-for-profits, those volunteers involved in development only can easily lose touch with the direction in which the rest of the organization is heading. It is important that a good effort be made to keep these volunteers informed. Why? Because the fund-raising volunteers are in closer touch with the general public than is anyone else in the organization. This more frequent contact with the public gives the development volunteers greater opportunity to talk about the mission of the organization. Therefore, the development officers must be informed and pass the information along to the volunteers.

If you represent only the development part of your organization, you should act as a conduit for the volunteers and donors to help them understand what is going on in the rest of your charity. In many cases you can be the healer, the teacher, even the cheerleader for your organization.

I represent development for a hospital, and I would describe my job with two analogies. First: the development officer is a cheerleader for the hospital. Second: the hospital can be likened to a first-class ocean liner. The captain is the administrator. He and his crew are responsible for the safety and comfort of the passengers (i.e., the patients). He must get them from port to port on time and provide an overall good experience during the voyage.

The development officer's job is to sell tickets for the trip. In this case, development is like a travel agency. We drum up business. We persuade people that they want to sail on our ship. With that in mind, I have always believed that in addition to raising funds for support of our hospital, we must make friends and educate the community about the advantages of sailing on our ship.

Another responsibility is learning to use the resources that are available to you. If you work for a large charity, your charity may have hundreds of employees just out of reach of your needs. How can you get those people to assist you in your quest? We instituted a program that we call the Employee Ambassadors Committee.

With consent of hospital management, we invited twenty-four of our hospital's employees to a meeting at which we asked them to join us in raising funds for the hospital. There were no senior management people invited. They were all rank-and-file employees. Happily, I can tell you that because of the Ambassadors Committee, we activated nearly all of our hospital's employees. Somewhere around 85 percent of them contribute a total of about $80,000 annually.

In any organization you have official managers, those paid to provide leadership, and you also have unofficial managers. The unofficial managers are often the long-term employees to whom many go to for advice on all manner of problems. If you're smart, you will identify these people and seek their help. Without them, any program you wish to establish with your employees will more than likely fail. With them, you can hit the proverbial home run every time.

Any development officer who believes that looking successful is to be successful is out of touch with reality. Nothing will turn off volunteers and donors more quickly than seeing their development officer sitting in a chair twice as big as theirs behind a mahogany desk, or driving a luxurious automobile. If you want to look successful, dress appropriately, be prepared, listen until you have something worth saying, and so on. You may be asking, what does this have to do with working within the system? The answer is: by being flashy or ostentatious, you run the risk of alienating the very people you need the most. The people that you would normally want to be your friends will not want anything to do with you. I have always viewed invitations from wealthy volunteers as a way for them to say, "Bill, you're doing a good job." I do not delude myself into thinking that I am a social equal to my wealthy volunteers or donors.

I hope you understand the message I am sending. I know of no one who is better than I, but I am not on a social par with the Queen of England or the President of the United States or some of the wealthy volunteers who on occasion invite my spouse and me to their homes.

Assess the resources that are readily available to you, and working within the system, use them to the best advantage of your charity.

Top Volunteers

Charities need all types of volunteers for all kinds of

jobs—envelope stuffers, typists, solicitors, organizers, and leaders. However, too many charities are timid about recruiting the rich, powerful, and influential volunteers. Recruiting the richest and most powerful volunteers available should be among the highest priorities for any charity. You want all types of people on your board and involved on your committees, including those who can bring with them wealth, power, and influence.

The question is how to get these volunteers to serve on your board. You may have to start with less powerful, less wealthy, less influential people, but that's okay! There are very few times in this life when you start with the best. Most of us buy a starter house and work up each time we sell. Sometimes, one very rich and powerful volunteer can turn an organization around. Just stay pointed in that direction. I will have more to say about recruiting volunteers in other chapters.

Other Responsibilities

Everyone wants to move up in job responsibility and pay. However, the proper use of your development staff is crucial to your success. Be fair to yourself; you can't make a silk purse out of a sow's ear. If you promote from within your current staff, be sure that the individual you promote has the tools to be successful. Provide that person with the proper training and support. If you are the manager, you owe that person every bit of assistance you can muster.

On the other hand, if out of blind loyalty you promote a person who doesn't have the training, talent, or ability and that individual fails, you will be held accountable.

Another responsibility is to stay within the organization's mission and major goals. What good is it to the organization if you have the finest health fair in the state if you work for an art museum?

Ethics

My career has given me the pleasure of working with some highly ethical people. I believe I'm the better for it. However, you can't be in development very long without either meeting or hearing of a scoundrel. The same is true of all professions. However, because we rely on the public's trust, it is of paramount importance to us to avoid even the appearance of unethical behavior.

In the early days of my career, I had the advantage of meeting a couple of pretty rotten apples. That was good for me because I recognized them for what they were and wanted to demonstrate that there were good people in fund raising, too. It may have, without my realizing it at the time, caused me to stress honesty more than I otherwise would have in my career.

Developing strong interpersonal, communication, and leadership skills is essential. For us to improve in these areas requires us to apply ourselves. Attend classes or identify a person who has a skill you particularly admire and seek that person's help. Asking for help is one of the greatest forms of flattery known to mankind. So don't hesitate to do it.

We should always be growing in our knowledge of successful fund-raising methods and in acquiring people managing skills, the financial knowledge, and organization skills that accompany them. All charities must recognize the benefit of training and provide the moral and financial support to encourage the staff to acquire it.

Other skills and responsibilities that staff should have include business management, leadership, financial, quantitative and statistical skills, and computer literacy.

A Long List

We have identified a long list of responsibilities and skills that a top-notch development officer should have. Yet, none of us can have all these qualities, no matter how smart or how great we are. That's one of the reasons we have volunteers. Recruit a volunteer who is strong in an area where you are weak.

Once, during an annual salary review, I was criticized for not being stronger in understanding the financial area of my charity. The irony is that our fund-raising had quadrupled in my first three years, we had exceeded our revenue goal each year by more than $100,000, and we had never exceeded our expenses. When I pointed this out, I heard later that I was now considered defensive.

I am not unique. This is the kind of comment that comes up in nearly every annual review. Just remember that not many people have the capacity to praise. Training in Total Quality Management seeks to overcome such lacks. I'm praying for rapid conversions.

A Fund-Raising Stew

As we come close to the end of Chapter 1, I would like to point out that not everything necessary for success in fund raising falls on the shoulders of the development officer. If charitable organizations are to be successful in fund raising, they need the following ingredients:

1. An institution that is providing a needed service, has good management, and has a successful track record.. A 501(c)(3) provided by the United States government.
3. A clear and concise Mission and Case Statement.
4. A fund-raising plan that parallels the institution's objectives.
5. Committed volunteers and staff.

These are ingredients of a good fund-raising stew.

We live in a world that is constantly changing. If we are to keep up, we too must be willing to change. The more realistic a charity is (that is, the more agreeable they are to allowing the continuing education and improvement of the skills of their volunteers and staff), the more likely they are to succeed.

Many charities want their development staff to know as much about fund raising as possible. They are willing to pay for the advanced training that is available at local or nearby colleges that offer courses in public speaking, computers, human relations, tax laws, finance, and management.

The Role of Staff

Development officers practice the art of fund raising in many different ways. The way you practice usually depends on several details: the way you entered the fund-raising profession, the training you have received since becoming a fund raiser, the supervision you have had, and what your supervisor expects from you. I have noticed that fund-raising professionals are a pretty unselfish lot. They seem willing to answer any questions asked of them and to help a novice in any way they can.

Fund Raising 101

Chapter Two

Professional Ethics

In this chapter, we briefly discuss ethical standards for fund raisers as professionals or as volunteers. The subject of professional ethics occurs in this book because ethical behavior is so very important to us in everything we do throughout our entire professional careers.

In the United States, charities have established a tradition of trust. The public believes that we will be there at their time of need. Without this trust, the effectiveness of charities would quickly vanish, the agreement that we have with society would be worthless, and the fabric of our mission would begin to unravel. As charities, we are completely dependent on the public's goodwill to reach our goals. We must do everything within our power to maintain that trust.

The average person contributes to your charity has the right to expect that you will do what you say you will do.

From an early age, we have been taught that a policeman can be trusted. Therefore, when you see the uniform of a policeman, you feel a certain amount of security. That same type of trust is extended to those of us who work with charities. We must go the extra mile, above and beyond the call of duty, to merit that trust. Like the policeman's uniform, charities are given a measure of respect without having to earn it. Simply by
existing, the work charities do is seen as an extension of the work the

public would like to see carried out. Every time some charity fails to live up to the public confidence, it hurts all of us.

My experience with people of little, or no ethics, has been somewhat limited. You might say that I've been lucky. However, while working with a national charity, I discovered through an audit that one of the fifty or so directors I was supervising had her hand in the cookie jar. We dealt with it quickly, and the chapter didn't suffer any long-term ill effects. Nevertheless, because of this one individual, the entire charity was made vulnerable for that brief time.

Because of the 1992 in the headquarters of United Way of America. United Way chapters all across the United States are still being punished for one man's misuse of his authority. If the United Way were only a name and if there were no people behind the name, it wouldn't be so bad. But the United Way's funds represent battered women and children, the Red Cross, mentally and physically handicapped people, legal services, and on and on.

When one of us errs, the error stains all of us. The confidence and trust earned by those who came before us, as well as the confidence and trust that we have earned, are weakened. We must be aboveboard at all times, be out in plain view, take action to see that our projects and programs are efficient, and that they meet their stated purposes. We must institute quality control measures and be accountable to our donors and ourselves. We must also be outspoken when we become aware of behavior that is improper.

Although we were appalled by the actions of the individual who caused this dark cloud to come over American charities, my chapter of the National Society of Fund Raising Executives issued a vote of confidence for our local United Way chapter. The work they do in the community is praiseworthy and deserves support from all sources.

NSFRE Code of Ethics

The following is the National Society of Fund Raising Executives Code of Ethical Principles and Standards of Professional Practice. The code is for members of NSFRE, and each member must sign a pledge to uphold it. The Society intends to enforce these standards through its national Ethics Committee. If you are not currently a member of the Society, I encourage you to join.

Code of Ethical Principles and Standards of Professional Practice
Statements of Ethical Principles
Adopted, November 1991

The National Society of Fund Raising Executives exists to foster the development and growth of fund-raising professionals and the profession, to preserve and enhance philanthropy and volunteerism, and to promote high ethical standards in the fund-raising profession.

To these ends, this code declares the ethical values and standards of professional practice which NSFRE members embrace and which they strive to uphold in their responsibilities for generating philanthropic support.

Members of the National Society of Fund Raising Executives are motivated by an inner drive to improve the quality of life through the causes they serve. They seek to inspire others through their own sense of dedication and high purpose. They are committed to the improvement of their professional knowledge and skills in order that their performance will better serve others. They recognize their stewardship responsibility to ensure that needed resources are vigorously and ethically sought and that the intent of the donor is honestly fulfilled. Such individuals practice their profession with integrity, honesty, truthfulness, and adherence to the absolute obligation to safeguard the public trust.

Furthermore, NSFRE members

*   serve the ideal of philanthropy, are committed to the preservation and enhancement of volunteerism, and hold

17

Fund Raising 101

stewardship of these concepts as the overriding principle of professional life;

* put charitable mission above personal gain, accepting compensation by salary or set fee only;

* foster cultural diversity and pluralistic values and treat all people with dignity and respect;

* affirm, through personal giving, a commitment to philanthropy and its role in society;

* adhere to the spirit as well as the letter of all applicable laws and regulations;

* bring credit to the fund-raising profession by their public demeanor;

* recognize their individual boundaries of competence and are forthcoming about their professional qualifications and credentials;

* value the privacy, freedom of choice, and interests of all those affected by their actions;

* disclose all relationships which might constitute, or appear to constitute, conflicts of interest;

* actively encourage all their colleagues to embrace and practice these ethical principles;

* adhere to the following standards of professional practice in their responsibilities for generating philanthropic support.

18

Standards of Professional Practice
Adopted and incorporated into the NSFRE Code of Ethical Principles
November 1992

1. Members shall act according to the highest standards and visions of their institution, profession, and conscience.

2. Members shall comply with all applicable local, state, provincial, and federal civil and criminal laws. Members should avoid the appearance of any criminal offense or professional misconduct.

3. Members shall be responsible for advocating, within their own organizations, adherence to all applicable laws and regulations.

4. Members shall work for a salary or fee, not percentage-based compensation or a commission.

5. Members may accept performance-based compensation such as bonuses provided that such bonuses are in accord with prevailing practices within the members' own organizations and are not based on a percentage of philanthropic funds raised.

6. Members shall neither seek nor accept finder's fees and shall, to the best of their ability, discourage their organizations from paying such fees.

7. Members shall disclose all conflicts of interest; such disclosure does not preclude or imply ethical impropriety.

8. Members shall accurately state their professional experience, qualifications, and expertise.

Fund Raising 101

9. Members shall adhere to the principle that all donor and prospect information created by, or on behalf of, an institution is the property of that institution and shall not be transferred or removed.

10. Members shall, on a scheduled basis, give donors the opportunity to have their names removed from lists which are sold to, rented to, or exchanged with other organizations.

11. Members shall not disclose privileged information to unauthorized parties.

12. Members shall keep constituent information confidential.

13. Members shall take care to ensure that all solicitation materials are accurate and correctly reflect the organization's mission and use of solicited funds.

14. Members shall, to the best of their ability, ensure that contributions are used in accordance with donors intentions.

15. Members shall ensure, to the best of their ability, proper stewardship of charitable contributions, including: careful investment of funds; timely reports on the use and management of funds; and explicit consent by the donor before altering the conditions of a gift.

16. Members shall ensure, to the best of their ability, that donors receive informed and ethical advice about the value and tax implications of potential gifts.
jlh 3/20/93

Chapter Three

The Role of Volunteers

Webster's *Dictionary* says that a volunteer is "one who enters or offers himself for a service of his own free will." To me, Webster's description falls pitifully short as a description of volunteerism and the volunteer spirit. In 1987, while conducting a capital campaign for St. Francis Regional Medical Center in Wichita, Kansas, I felt the need for a catchphrase for the hospital auxiliary. They had just committed a substantial gift requiring a good deal of sacrifice from their organization to the capital campaign.

While thinking about it, I remembered that nurses are often described as the heart of a hospital. I reasoned that the doctors might be thought of as the hands and that the administration could be considered the brain. (I realize that this one statement could spark a debate of gigantic proportion. A friend, himself a hospital administrator, who collects oxymorons would say, "Hospital administrators and brains is the ultimate oxymoron"). Back to the subject at hand, the auxiliary. What then could the auxiliary be? I thought about it for two or three days, and finally it hit me. The auxiliary is the smile. And many times since then, while working with various charities, I have thought of their volunteers as the smile of their organization.

Volunteers come in all shapes and sizes, all religions, creeds, colors, and sexes. They come from all walks of life; professional, blue collar, homemakers, even Indian chiefs. They are rich or poor or somewhere in between. They are big or little or some variation of one of these. Volunteers can be anything and can be found everywhere.

It has been said that one of the things that makes the United States so unique is the volunteer sector. I have found that volunteerism in each community is also one of the largest contributors to the personality of that community. If you should have the misfortune of moving into a community that is cold to its citizenry, you are apt to discover that volunteerism is absent. A good and recent example is Hurricane Hugo in 1992. As it retreats into our collective memories, I suspect the winds will become stronger and the devastations even more onerous. Each person directly involved will have a story to share about the difficulties experienced or the heroism witnessed.

I know that I will never forget the devastation that CNN and other broadcasters laid out for the world to see. Etched in my memory are the pictures of entire communities knocked to the ground and people wandering the streets looking for loved ones.

Throughout the days and nights that followed, it seemed that for every call for help there was someone calling to volunteer assistance. Hundreds, even thousands, of people drove or flew to south Florida to lend a hand. They carried all the blankets and fresh water allowed. I don't believe I've ever witnessed more genuine concern or greater willingness to help neighbors in need.

Even more impressive was that the intent of the help was unconditional. Assistance was given to all, whether they were aids-infected or healthy, black or white, straight or gay. At least in the early days, the issues that drive us apart were set aside while we worked on the common problem. There's nothing quite like a crisis to bring the American people together in the spirit of true volunteerism.

Maximizing Volunteer Effort

22

The Role of Volunteers

If you plan to use volunteers in your organization, there are several things you should do to maximize their effort. To keep from wasting their time, have a specific job for each volunteer to do and, if possible, write a job description for the duty being assigned. With more than 100 volunteer leaders and chairmen in our organization and with constant changes, we are not able to have job descriptions for every single task, but we do have them for most.

By way of organization, we have agendas for all meetings, keep minutes, and work from time lines. We coordinate work schedules, often working out specific priorities with each volunteer leader. Because time is such a precious commodity to quality volunteers, it is imperative that you (1) have a method for measuring results, (2) schedule according to the volunteers' availability, and (3) provide the necessary clerical support to see that the volunteers look and feel prepared.

Why Would You Want to have Volunteers?

A good volunteer program has many benefits. You have a pool of trained volunteers standing by, ready to ascend to various chairs and boards where you need good trained committed leaders. Your charity will receive many residual benefits from this involvement, such as an increased level of contributions and volunteer hours.

Where Do You Find Volunteers?

You can find volunteers by looking at various membership lists, including the local country clubs, chambers of commerce, city directories, bank trustees, civic clubs. Even the society section of your newspaper can become a source of names of prospective volunteers.

The best place to find volunteers is by asking your current volunteers to suggest people they know or have worked with who would be an asset to your charity.

The Role of Volunteers

Fund Raising 101

Everything that the volunteer does for a charity is important. It would be impossible for me to identify one thing that is more important than another. However, some activities are the exclusive responsibility of volunteers and should not fall on the shoulders of the staff.

Chief among these is **setting policy and determining strategic direction for the charity**. Other key areas of volunteer involvement include fund raising and hiring the charity's executive director. And most certainly, the volunteers should approve the mission of the charity and its goals and objectives. These are the primary responsibilities of the volunteers. Anything else is either the responsibility of the staff or is shared by volunteers and staff.

The Value of Volunteers

Dedicated and committed volunteers are the key ingredient necessary for a charity to have a long-lasting success. The reasons they are a key factor include the following:

1. Wealthy and powerful volunteers have more contacts throughout the community than almost any development.
2. The involvement of such people validates the charity.
3. They can afford to provide substantial financial support.
4. A volunteer making a case for your charity to a prospective donor increases your charity's credibility tenfold in the mind of the prospect.

Training for Volunteers

Every volunteer has a unique history and a variety of individual skills. However, in spite of their background, even wealthy and powerful people need training. Some may have received part or much of this training while working with other charities. Yet, it would be smart for you to evaluate where each volunteer is on the learning curve and what you must do by way of training to bring them up to the proficiency you are seeking. A questionnaire to help you evaluate volunteers is at the end of this chapter.

The Role of Volunteers

Every day more training tools are being made available to assist you. After you have evaluated each volunteer, expose them to specific training. I have used portions of books that address volunteer responsibilities. I have used videos that teach volunteers how to ask for a major gift. I have used speakers who covered aspects of cooperation among volunteers. And I have used personality quizzes to demonstrate the differences within our group.

Proper orientation can be helpful in training volunteers, and a good manual can provide the answers to many frequently asked questions. The following is a list of the various subjects that we include in our orientation manual. Each board member, volunteer chair, and subcommittee chair receives a copy of the manual.

1. A roster of board members with their home and business addresses and phone numbers
2. Organizational charts
3. Identity of all committees with chair and members
4. A list of all scheduled meetings
5. Mission statement
6. A capsule history of the development office
7. Names of development office staff
8. Responsibilities of board members
9. A list of all major current and future projects
10. Annual Plan and Ten-Year Plan
11. Samples of important newspaper articles and other information about the charity
12. By-laws — if you have them
13. A fact sheet about the charity
14. Map and other pertinent data
15. A section for minutes
16. A section for finance reports

In many states, volunteers are legally accountable for all activities that they oversee through the planning and the evaluating functions. Therefore, if you practice fund raising in one of those states, it is your responsibility to know if your volunteers are at risk and to inform them accordingly.

The Three W's

I try to recruit volunteers who meet the test of the Three Ws (Wealth, Wisdom, and Work). That is, they are wealthy, the community recognizes their wisdom, and they are willing to work for the charity's good. Most charities depend on the volunteers for securing adequate financial resources to meet the goals and objectives of the charity. They certainly need volunteers who are willing to think, work, and contribute. Hence, the Three Ws!

How Do You Motivate Volunteers?

I am a firm believer in the Golden Rule, "Do unto others as you would have them do unto you!" Plus, I love it when someone treats me special. And I want people to be honest with me. I use these three principles as a guide for the way I treat volunteers. I hope to create an atmosphere that is part civic club and part country club. My goal is to have everyone who passes through our doors to have fun and feel that they are contributing to a worthwhile cause.

On the front door of our foundation there is a sign that reads, "Through these doors pass the world's best volunteers." I carefully picked the two secretaries who meet and greet every person who enters our office. They have naturally friendly personalities, and I encourage them to use them. Everyone in our office makes a point of offering every visitor coffee or a soft drink. Our volunteers are provided an office that is identical to the others within our office suite. It is exclusively for our volunteers and no one else. I tell each volunteer that the entire office suite and staff are there to assist them and that they should call on us accordingly. Our volunteers have responded by providing quality, commitment, and unselfish leadership in their projects and programs.

Recognition of Volunteers

In 1992, the estimated dollar value of volunteer time in the

The Role of Volunteers

United States exceeded $150 billion. No doubt your charity received some of that time. Therefore, you and your charity must accept the responsibility of seeing that adequate appreciation and recognition are given to each volunteer.

Appreciation and recognition come in many forms. Examples are handwritten notes or gifts when appropriate (flowers, plants, plaques, etc.). These mementos can be given to worthy volunteers at special award and recognition ceremonies. Another way to recognize volunteers is through news releases to the local media. Also available from many charities are free passes to various events, discounts at a charity's retail store, and special parking.

Gratitude and a sense of belonging are two personality needs that nearly everyone craves. Recognition and appreciation are two ways to address these attributes. My old friend Bill Snell told me many years ago that 2 percent of a charity's gross revenue should be allocated for recognition and appreciation of volunteers and donors. At the time, Bill was a representative of a donor recognition company. But I'm *sure* he wouldn't have exaggerated. All kidding aside, it is commonly felt that from 1 to 2 percent of a charity's gross income should be allocated for appreciation and recognition of donors and volunteers.

For many years, the volunteer auxiliaries of hospitals have used pins as a recognition tool. Having been active in the U.S. Jaycee organization for some time, I am one of the leftover Jaycee pin traders, sometimes referred to as "Pin Hacks."

We use pins to promote our hospital foundation right now. We have a pin for our employee volunteers as well as for any employee who contributes through payroll deduction to our foundation. They wear them on their ID badges. We have another pin for those who contribute to the Children's Miracle Network Telethon and still another for people who put the foundation in their will. As you can tell, we are big on pins and feel they have contributed to elevating the number of employees who contribute to the foundation.

Fund Raising 101

Because volunteers are so important to any not-for-profit organization, we must make an effort to show our gratitude for the work and dedication they exhibit. Foremost in the volunteer's mind is succeeding at the task that they have accepted. It is likely that others succeeded in the same task in prior years, and no one wishes to be the first to not reach the goal.

Evidence of this concern is exhibited each year by our Black-Tie Gala chairwoman. The moment the person accepts the chair, the realization hits her that everyone is depending on her for a successful gala. To ensure that she measures up to last year's success, the new chair begins meeting with the committees earlier than the previous chair did. I admire their willingness to dig in and do whatever is necessary to succeed.

I close this chapter on volunteerism with a quotation from John Kenneth Galbraith: "Every community needs a great many services. To pay for them is expensive; and only a poor class of talent is available for money. By rewarding volunteer workers with gifts of honor and esteem, the very best people can be had for nothing."

A Questionnaire for New Volunteers

Following are the questions that I ask new volunteers:

1. Have you been a volunteer with other charities?
2. What were the charities with which you served?
3. What volunteer roles did you have with each charity?
4. Did you enjoy your roles in the other charities?
5. Did you feel that your talents and interests were properly used in those roles?
6. While involved with our charity, would you like to serve in similar positions, or would you prefer new challenges?
7. If new challenges, where would your interests lie?
8. Do you enjoy fund-raising activities and projects?
9. Are you aware of the various projects that we conduct to raise funds?

The Role of Volunteers

10. Is there a particular project that you are interested in becoming involved with?
11. Do you feel that recognition of volunteers is important?
12. If done in good taste and not excessive, will you participate in recognition when appropriate?
13. Is there anything that we should have asked that you believe would be beneficial for us to know?

Fund Raising 101

Chapter Four

Boards
and Committees

Having a large number of volunteers can be a blessing or a curse. They are a blessing when YOU are properly prepared to manage them. We will help you eliminate the curse by defining the responsibilities and the organization of boards and their various committees.

The Board's Broad Responsibilities
The responsibilities of a board member fall into the following five broad categories:
1. They provide contacts and influence.
2. They serve as fiduciary agents, legally responsible for all activities. They are expected to act as "reasonably prudent persons."
3. They approve annual goals and objectives, monitor progress against goals and objectives, serve as program overseers, review program recommendations, adding, changing, and deleting when appropriate.
4. As evaluators they determine strengths, weaknesses, successes, and failures. They recommend changes for better performance, and they work with the staff as partners.

5.   They are responsible for monitoring the dispersement of the funds in accordance with the institutions' goals.

It can help you to remember this one phrase: **the staff manages and the board governs.** That's how it should work in the volunteer sector.

Relationships Between Staff and Volunteers

The best relationship occurs when the board and the staff both understand their different roles. They should be members of the same team, and each should consider the other to be as essential as they believe themselves to be. Sometimes I've described this relationship as 50/50, a marriage, or a partnership.

Avoid secrecy. Although the board has the right to conduct executive sessions, they should avoid them like the plague. The moment the board goes into an executive session, trust from the development staff flies out the window.

There is never a sufficiently good reason to exclude the executive director from executive committee meetings. I'm sure you understand that I'm not talking about the occasional annual review or personnel discipline. But these should be the exception rather than the rule. Ideally, communications should be open and honest, with each keeping the other informed.

I once had a chairman who told me that he would be my eyes and ears in the community. In two years he never gave me a positive statement. He had plenty of negative comments but never a positive one. You can imagine how much I enjoyed those two years. In spite of tremendous volunteer recruitment and financial success, all he could comment on were the times we didn't dot the I or cross the T. I don't think this man really meant any harm, but because of his profession, he had spent his entire life isolating problems and solving them. He had no background or experience in finding a success and reveling in it. You need and want volunteers who dream of something better and are willing to work for it.

Recruiting Volunteers for Boards

Throughout my career, I have recruited hundreds of

32

Boards and Committees

volunteers. Many of them were recruited for involvement in a specific project. Others were recruited to serve on a board. This section concentrates on volunteers for boards. A good and effective board is so important that I have tried to evaluate the good ones to determine if they contained some sort of magic ingredient. Alas, I regret to say that I have never been able to put my finger on that illusive magic ingredient.

However, a commonality existed in most of the successful boards that I helped to build. These boards seem to have achieved more confidence in their collective ability if they were assembled in a logical order. Because of this, I have developed a method that I believe will be helpful to you as you assemble your boards and committees.

A dream board in your community might look something like figure 1. Remember to keep the Three W's (Wealth, Wisdom, and Work) in mind. You also want a cross section of the various professionals and leaders of small businesses and large corporations, as well as influential and wealthy individuals. And three other things to consider are race, sex, and religion. With all this in mind, consider that a twenty-five member board might have some of the following representations: (See Figure 1)   This grading scale is based on how well people of the various occupations who are volunteers have worked with me during my twenty-five years of working with volunteers. Naturally, a really good volunteer can come from any profession or walk of life. Members of some groups are generally not your best workers, however.

Using the same listed occupations, I might put a board together as shown in figure 2: (See figure 2)

The twenty-five I've chosen represent professions I have had particularly good results with, especially the ones with more than one representative. The professions with only one representative and the CPA categories are needed professions because of their specific expertise—for example, architects, insurance salespersons, real estate salespersons. As a rule, bankers, attorneys, and friends of the charity are the categories that have always worked the hardest for the

Figure 1

Architect	B		
Attorneys	B		
Auto Dealers	B		
Bankers	A		
Contractors	C	Grading scale	
CPAs	B	A	Terrific
Homemaker/Civic Leader	A	B	Very good
Hotel/Motel Manager	B	C	Poor
Insurance Sales	B		
Large Corporation CEO	B		
Physicians/Dentists	C		
Real Estate Sales	B		
Retirees	A		
Small Business Owners	B		
Your Charity's Friends	A		

charities I've been associated with. Friends of the charity are defined as those volunteers who believe in the charity and its goals. They worked even when no one else was.

As I mentioned earlier, I am employed by a hospital. When I arrived at the hospital, I found a small group of volunteers who were relatively eager to see their foundation become successful. This was the first time that I didn't follow my own advice and set up a training regimen. Later, I regretted it.

When I arrived, my foundation had a board of twenty-five and two annual special events with approximately seventy-five volunteers. Five years later, we have grown to approximately thirty-five committees and subcommittees. Our black-tie event has a steering committee made up of seven officers and 18 subcommittees representing another 90 volunteers. There are hundreds of additional volunteers involved with our telethon and its associated events.

The Telethon Steering Committee is made up of chairpersons from each of the following committees: the Duck Race, Advance

Boards and Committees

Figure 2

Architect	(1)
Attorneys	(2)
Auto Dealers	(2)
Bankers	(2)
Contractors	(1)
CPAs	(2)
Homemaker/Civic Leaders	(2)
Hotel/Motel Managers	(1)
Insurance Sales	(1)
Large Corporation CEO	(3)
Physicians/Dentists	(1)
Real Estate Sales	(1)
Retirees	(2)
Small Business Owners	(2)
Your Charity's Friends	(2)

Gifts, Phon-a-Thon, Balloons, Stars Come Out for Christmas, Celebrate, and the Special Programs Committee.

When the members of the Nominating Committee, the Finance Committee, Investment/Personnel Committee, Cancer Advisory Committee, the Physicians Advisory Group for Endowment, the Professional Advisory Committee, and any number of ad hoc committees are added, the number of volunteers becomes quite substantial. Examples of the latter are a road block, car wash, and the like.

Recommended Committees

Committees are the structures normally used to provide order when hundreds of volunteers are involved. By using committees, a relatively small group of volunteers and staff will be able to manage the business of a very active charity.

I recommend chairpersons for all fund-raising events as well as for program events. And don't overlook the logic for having chairpersons for major geographic areas. When I started with the

35

Fund Raising 101

March of Dimes, I recruited a chairperson and treasurer for each county in the southern half of Arkansas. By using one or the other of these volunteer leaders as a starting point, I built a county organization that conducted fund-raising and program events.

Charities often have to use whatever resources and manpower are available to them. Following is a list of the committees I consider to be ideal for an organization located in one city. I will list them together and follow with an explanation of each.

1. Finance
2. Development
   - 2a Annual or Current
   - 2b Planned
   - 2c Special Events
   - 2d Capital
   - 2e Grants
3. Personnel
4. Investment
5. Programs
   - 5a Police liaison
   - 5b Elementary school representative
6. Nominating/Manpower

These committees are what I consider to be standing committees. They, along with ad hoc and subcommittees, meet and work out details, time lines, budgets, and so on. The various chairpersons of the committees report at the executive committee meetings and request board approval of their plans. Upon approval, the committee chairs and the staff activate the project or program.

The charity's staff should be responsible for creating a reporting system between the volunteers, the committee chairs, and the board executive committee. The staff should also write job descriptions and time lines for each volunteer layer and for each project. The Annual Plan and the Five-Year Plan, which are discussed in Chapter 7, should identify the types of projects and programs and their manpower and other needs.

Boards and Committees

Developing the Right Committees

FINANCE COMMITTEE - The finance committee should have at least two CPAs and three businesspersons. As a group, they should understand the financial needs of the charity and how to budget revenue and expenses accordingly. Naturally, the executive director must work closely with the committee.

DEVELOPMENT - If your charity has fund raising as a responsibility, primary among these committees is the development committee. The development committee is charged with the responsibility of setting policy for fund raising. With approval of the executive committee, enlist volunteer leadership and workers and develop a comprehensive fund-raising plan that meets the financial goals and objectives and is compatible with the institution's strategic plan.

Although the staff may recommend a specific overall fund-raising goal as well as goals for each project, it is up to the development committee to understand and determine if the goals are reasonable. My personal feeling is that in this area, the executive director's recommendation should be given strong consideration.

Goals

Some fund-raising professionals and volunteers feel that a realistic and achievable goal is the way to go. Others feel that an unrealistic goal is better because even if you don't reach it, you will likely raise more money by trying.

I strongly recommend a challenging, reasonable goal. I know of nothing that is more discouraging than NOT to reach your goal. I have yet to meet the volunteer who didn't believe he or she had failed by not meeting the appointed target. I've been able to explain this logic to my volunteer leadership and have almost always received their cooperation and compliance.

When Looking for Volunteers

Remember, if you are truly a volunteer organization, volunteers will occupy the critical roles in the planning and implementation of all fund-raising projects. Look for the following leadership qualities: (1) they must be willing to challenge the committee members with both personal generosity and willingness to work, (2) they must be respected by their peers, (3) they must be flexible, and (4) they must be willing to ask for gifts.

Development committee members are often the wealthiest and most powerful individuals in the community. They can be corporate or business executives or other wealthy leaders.

Staff Functions

The staff members working with the development committee have a responsibility: to provide support and information to the committee concerning the needs for manpower, supplies, training, and managing the day-to-day development function.

A well-formed and matured development program will incorporate all types of giving projects including annual gifts, planned giving gifts, special event projects, capital campaigns, and grant writing.

The staff usually present the committee with a draft of a plan that incorporates as many fund-raising projects as they feel they have manpower and resources to manage successfully. They will suggest timing as well as the individuals that they feel will make good chairpersons and maybe even some committee members.

The development committee and staff discuss the suggestions and together arrive at a final plan. Once the plan has been approved by the executive committee, the chairs begin the recruitment of the needed volunteers. Training for these new volunteers should follow shortly.

PERSONNEL - The personnel committee has three primary responsibilities. First, when asked to do so by the charity's board chairperson, they conduct the search for a new executive director. Second, if the executive director has any interest in making organizational changes, they hear the recommendations and discuss the changes, giving the executive director the benefit of any expertise they have. Third, they see to it that the executive director receives a fair and equitable hearing should his or her leadership be challenged.

The personnel committee should not interfere with the executive director's responsibility to hire, fire, or otherwise discipline his or her own staff. If a problem arises between the executive director and another employee, the executive director may ask this committee to act as a mediator.

INVESTMENT - Not every charity has or even needs an investment committee. But if you have an endowment or other funds that accumulate, the executive director should have a group of at least three volunteers with investment experience to make investment decisions. If your organization is located in a large community, it will not be a problem for you to find well-qualified people to advise you in this area. In smaller communities, you can secure this type of help from banks or local entrepreneurs who have a good track record in the stock and bond markets.

PROGRAMS - All charities have some sort of program for their constituency. For example, hospitals often provide health fairs, and Junior Achievement conducts public school programs in economics. Smaller charities, such as a small museum, may be receiving rent-free space and need funds only to pay for their exhibits. In fact, they wouldn't raise funds at all if not for their exhibits. Therefore, it is logical to recruit good volunteers who excel at this type of community involvement.

The charity's executive director may develop a draft of a plan and present it to the volunteers for whatever additions, deletions, or corrections that might be necessary. Once this step is completed and approved by the executive committee, the plan is put into action by the volunteers and staff.

NOMINATING and MANPOWER - The Nominating and Manpower Committee is responsible for the identification and recruitment of volunteers to join the charity's board or committees. Often, the place to start in recruiting volunteers is to evaluate the previous years' volunteers. Ask the good ones if they have a friend or friends whom they would like to involve in the charity's work.

They will often provide names. If your volunteers have been correctly evaluated concerning their interest and skills, work assignments can be easily made and you are on your way.

Selecting the Right Person to Chair

Recruiting a chairperson can often make or break a project. Generally, you want a leader who can make significant gifts or solicit them or both. It is always helpful if the chairperson is well known and respected in the community, has personal characteristics that make him or her an asset to your organization, is among the most difficult people to say no to, and is willing to make your organization a high priority.

Where Do You Find Volunteers?

Start with your board and remember that you want quality, not just names. Board members can make lists of the people they have worked with in other organizations, gone to church with, or maybe know at their place of employment.

It's not unusual to find good volunteers in the society columns of your newspaper. Businesses new to your community are great sources for volunteers. Don't overlook service organizations such as Rotary, Kiwanis, Jaycees, and Junior Leagues. Young people in area high schools and colleges often make excellent volunteers.

I have found volunteers in service companies such as banks, accounting firms, and law firms. Remember, these types of businesses have a large clientele that they can also involve in your projects.

Orderly Meetings

I'm going to close this chapter by discussing meetings and enclosing an example of an agenda.

Everyone agrees that having a regular meeting date and time is important. It allows everyone involved to plan accordingly. The meeting itself should also include regular committee chair reports. In the case of the executive committee, they can accept or reject

Boards and Committees

reports or recommendations of the committee chairpersons. Meetings should always start on time and end as closely as possible at the predetermined time.

If committee members require reminders, the staff should be responsible for mailing them out in a timely manner. Staff should also provide the minutes of all previous and current committee meetings and handle the required follow-up on issues that come up during the meeting. (See Figure 3 for a sample agenda.)

Figure 3

ANYTOWN A.B.C. FOUNDATION, INC.
Executive Committee Meeting
Agenda
James A. Coltron, Chairman
February 11, 1993

I.	Call to Order	J. Coltron
II.	Invocation	J. Doe
III.	Minutes*	J. Coltron
IV.	Committee and Other Reports	
	A. Financial*	M. Morris
	B. Development	L. Kennedy
	C. Black Tie Event	M. Taylor
	D. Telethon	J. Burkett
	E. Planned Giving	C. Lock
	G. Professional Advisory Committee	C. Fortner
	H. Major Gift Planning	J. Highcourt
	I. Parent Board	C. Bishop
V.	Old and New Business	
	A. Auto Lease	Staff
	B. Last minute items	
VI.	Announcements	Anyone
VII.	Adjourn	

* Requires approval of the Executive Committee

Fund Raising 101

Chapter Five

The Cultivation of Donors

What is the most common mistake that inexperienced fund raisers make? Whether volunteer or professional, they usually bypass most of the more important steps, that's what. They just drop in on the prospect and ask for a gift. That often is all that is needed to secure some financial support. The problem with this approach is that it rarely results in more than a minimal gift.

Nearly everything in life follows a logical and progressive set of steps to a conclusion. It then stands to reason that the cultivation of donors would likewise follow some logical procedure. Among fund-raising professionals, it is commonly felt that there are seven logical steps in donor relations, as follows:

1. Identification and research
2. Rating and evaluating
3. Cultivation
4. Involvement
5. Asking for the investment
6. Acknowledgment
7. Recognition

Fund Raising 101

Step 1 - Identification and Research

The donor cultivation process begins with the identification of those individuals and companies that should be considered your charity's constituency. Once you have identified the constituency, you need to know as much as possible about each prospect and rate them in priority so that you can call first on the ones with the greatest potential.

As much as we all wish it were true, not every wealthy person is a constituent of our charity. To determine your constituency, you must define those groups your charity serves. In the case of a college or university, you could consider your constituency to be students, their parents, their grandparents, companies who sell supplies and materials to the college, and certain businesses of the community that benefit simply because the college exists. For example, the nearby banking industry benefits if the local college has a very good banking program and graduates top-notch students. Likewise, if the local college has a medical program, the medical community therefore becomes part of its constituency. A good case can also be made for other businesses because of the ripple effect that a college's expenditures has on the community.

While conducting a capital campaign for a private college preparatory school in Jackson, Mississippi, a few years ago, we were able to go outside of our clear-cut constituency and convince a large real estate magnate to contribute $1 million to the school. This particular prep school was delivering a quality of education not thought to be otherwise available in the Jackson area. If Jackson was to attract top-level businesses and business managers to the community, this level of education had to be available for these people's children. That premise was strong enough to this particular real estate magnate to cause him, in his own self-interest, to invest in a school that he had no other reason to support.

Let's look at another example of constituency. Most national charities, such as the American Heart Association, the National Foundation March of Dimes, and the American Lung Association, have broad public appeal. We cannot be certain that we or our loved ones are not going to be victims of a heart attack or heart disease. Nor can we be certain that we or someone we love will not have a birth defect or fall prey to lung disease. These organizations raise great sums of monies through their efforts to cure major diseases and afflictions.

A little closer to home we could examine smaller charities such as homes for the handicapped, and the mentally ill, or an orphanage. These charities have a fairly broad base of appeal because they serve a segment of the community for which we all have compassion. The phrase "There, but for the grace of God, go I" frequently comes to mind.

My Rotary Club wanted to raise $100,000 in support of the International Rotary Foundation. This is a classic example of limited appeal. The funds raised by this project were to be sent to the Rotary Foundation, located outside of our community and maybe even used outside of the United States. Few, if any, local citizens would be inspired to support this fund raiser. Therefore, our constituency was limited to our membership. We did raise the $100,000.

Research should take the form of a three- to five-member committee made up of individuals who are extremely knowledgeable about the financial capability of people in the community. For this committee to avoid the tag of a rating committee, we call it the research and assessment committee.

Every charity could benefit from a research and assessment committee, and I highly recommend that you establish one. The purpose of this committee is to systematically learn everything that can be learned about your prospective donors. You will want to know routine information such as name, address, and place of employment. Also, not so routine information, such as where they attended college, if they inherited wealth, thrie place of worship, where they bank, and so on.

If you look over the following example carefully, it's easy to see how this information would be helpful when you are ready to call on the individual for a gift. Your group should be able to estimate key information such as the potential giving limits of the prospect,

Fund Raising 101

what types of property they hold (appreciated assets such as inherited property), and who is most likely to succeed on a solicitation call.

Example (You should lay this form out to suit your needs.)

Figure 4

Prospect Data

* Name: Work Phone:
* Working Address:
* City: State: Zip:
* Secretary:
* Spouse: Home Phone:
* Home Address:
* City: State:
* Zip:
* Children's names and ages:
* College information:
* Parent information:
* Place of worship:
* Are we aware of any special holdings of this individual or the family? (for example, appreciated property)
* Company's association with our organization other than as donor:
* Does company have matching gift program?
* Vendor to our charity:
* Who on our board or committee knows the contact?
* Gift history to our charity:
* To other charities:
* Research and assessment committee recommends: $
* Best call strategy:

The Cultivation of Donors

Step 2 - Rating and Evaluating

This step can also be accomplished by the research and assessment committee. All that we want to accomplish here is to agree on a reasonable dollar amount for the prospective donor to be asked to consider.

Rating or evaluating a prospect is the first place where the researched information is used. If you have a good estimate of a prospect's giving limits and if you have a good idea of where the gift is likely to come from (current income, appreciated property, or savings), then you will be able to estimate the amount donors can be asked to consider by the person making the call.

By now, you should be able to see why having the right people on the research and assessment committee is so helpful. If you know the prospect's place of worship, country club, civic club, and other data, you should not only be able to suggest an asking amount; you should be able to know who the right person is to make the solicitation call.

Step 3 - Cultivation

Cultivation of prospective donors begins as soon as an individual is identified as a prospective donor and can be accomplished in a variety of ways. Many charities mail newsletters to inform prospects of what the institution is all about. Others hold open houses or informal information meetings at a volunteer's home, where thoughtful discussions concerning the charity's mission take place or a representative from the institution speaks.

On occasion, articles from local newspapers are reproduced and mailed to prospects. The marketing department or a knowledgeable employee can write a white paper and it can be forwarded to prospects. And finally, one of the best ways to cultivate prospective donors is to encourage people who benefit by the charity's work to write or speak on the charity's behalf.

Step 4 - Involvement

Let's assume that one of the people who received some

information from you about your charity called or wrote to you asking for more information. This is your first opportunity for involvement. Anyone interested enough to write or call you is, as they say in the sales field, "a hot prospect."

Give the information requested and follow up with a phone call asking for a meeting. As soon as possible, assess the person's interest, and attempt to find an opportunity for her or him to get involved as a volunteer.

Involvement can be on a committee that is passing out information at a local mall. It can be as a tour guide within your institution. It can be stuffing envelopes. Anything that causes the person to become involved at a level that makes it clear that he or she is contributing to your charity.

Step 5 - Asking for the Investment

If the person who has been identified as a prospect has been rated, cultivated, and become involved, you have achieved a major part of your goal. Now all you need to do is have the right person ask for the investment. You have turned their gift into an investment in the charity's future. They already know what your charity is about because of the cultivation. They understand how it works from their involvement. They are ready to invest in its future.

I haven't deluded myself into thinking that everyone who reads this book will go through the seven steps every time they approach a prospect for a gift, but if you did, receiving larger gifts would become more common for you than for those who do not go through the steps.

There is a logical method of calling on a prospect and asking for the gift. That method follows in Chapter 8 titled, "How You Ask Makes the Difference".

Step 6 - Acknowledgment of the Gift

This step is often referred to as the first step in the process of securing your *next* gift from this donor.

Acknowledgments should be mailed out as soon as possible.

48

The Cultivation of Donors

Our goal is to send out the acknowledgment the same day that we receive the gift. However, we have a standing rule that we always mail out acknowledgments within forty-eight hours. If you wait longer than that, you are not placing enough emphasis on this important piece of your donor cultivation. The acknowledgment usually is in the form of a thank-you letter or card. It also indicates the amount the donor contributed so that the donor can be assured that you received the intended gift.

In January 1993 our foundation received a gift of $1,000 from a banking system that has branches in our community. Our records didn't show an outstanding pledge from this institution. I happened to know the president of the system, so I called him. I explained to him that, although we were a charity in need of revenue, we didn't wish to take money under false or accidental circumstances. I explained that we had received a check for $1,000 from his bank and that we didn't show an outstanding pledge. I further explained that maybe, in the confusion that takes place at year end, we inadvertently received some other charity's gift.

The president complimented me on my honesty and indicated that he would get back to me. An hour later he called and said that he wanted our charity to keep the gift in honor of the integrity exhibited by our charity. He further instructed me to relay to my boss what had occurred, and said that my boss should give me a pat on the back.

Needless to say, I did pass along that information about the surprise gift, but I left out the pat on the back. All I really did is what any ethical fund raiser should have done.

Step 7 - Recognition

Often-used recognition tools include the charity's magazine or newsletter, a donor wall where names of donors are placed according to the size of their contribution, and ads in local newspapers displaying names of donors. We have used these three in our foundation. We list all memorial and honorarium gifts in our hospital's quarterly magazine. We have a donor wall for the names of those donors who contributed to our last capital campaign, and the local newspaper generously denotes a double truck ad (two full pages) to the names of those contributing to our black-tie event.

Other events that we conduct allow for other opportunities for recognition. Our duck race has four Top Duck sponsors. They include a major bottling company, a radio station, a television station, and an automobile dealer. Each of the Top Duck sponsors contributes $10,000 or more in cash or in-kind support, and we display their logo on the 2,000-plus tee shirts and hats that we sell, on the 25,000 duck adoption papers that we distribute throughout the eighteen counties that we serve, and on the program booklet that is distributed to 52,000 area homes.

Motivations That Cause Individuals or Businesses to Give

People contribute to charities for many reasons. Some contribute for the influence that being a contributor to a certain charity brings them. If the gift is large enough, they can sometimes dictate the exact use of the contribution. Charities must be mindful of this reason for giving and not allow the donors to cause the charity to deviate from its mission.

Another reason for giving is to gain approval. A donor may not have the best reputation in a community. By contributing and being involved with popular charities, the donor uses financial clout in an attempt to enter the mainstream of a community's social set.

Another reason for giving can be a true desire to help. This reason may have come about because earlier the charity helped the donor or someone close to the donor. The donor may have the desire to help because he or she feels a sense of debt to the community. This was the reason a fellow agreed to chair a capital campaign I was involved with in Anniston, Alabama. A wealthy and powerful businessman's name came up over and over during the feasibility study. He had never really done anything for the community, yet he had several businesses that were prospering. The leadership of the charity in which I was engaged called on this man to serve in a leadership position for the campaign and told him, "You have

The Cultivation of Donors

enjoyed a lot of support from this community and you have never given back." He agreed with the statement and accepted the challenge. In fact, he was honored to be asked, made a significant lead gift, and served with great distinction.

Taxes are occasionally the motivation for an individual to make a contribution to a charity. There have been very few times that someone gave to a charity in which I was involved for tax reasons only. They were grateful for whatever tax breaks they received, but that's all.

At the end of 1992, my foundation came very close to receiving a charitable uni-trust funded by the sale of an apartment complex. The potential donor had absolutely no detectable charitable intent — at least none that I could see. Because of this lack, at the last moment he backed out. He wasn't sure he couldn't do better by selling and buying commercial annuities. If your potential donors do not have charitable intent, you're not going to get many gifts, including planned gifts.

Naturally, there are many other reasons for contributing to charities. Let your imagination run wild.

The Pyramid of Giving

If bread is the staff of life, then the pyramid of giving is the staff of giving. It is essential for fund-raising professionals to understand the pyramid of giving. Don't worry, it's not too complicated; it's just important.

The pyramid is an illustration that shows how new donors are brought into the charity through their small gifts and are promoted up the pyramid by using the seven logical steps of donor cultivation. After they are identified and the research has been conducted, they are evaluated. The cultivation through education begins and before they know it they are involved. Before they can turn around, their best friend is asking them to invest in your charity. They are promptly thanked, and all sorts of recognition are appearing all over the place.

See there, you knew all of that! Most of fund raising is common courtesy and common sense.

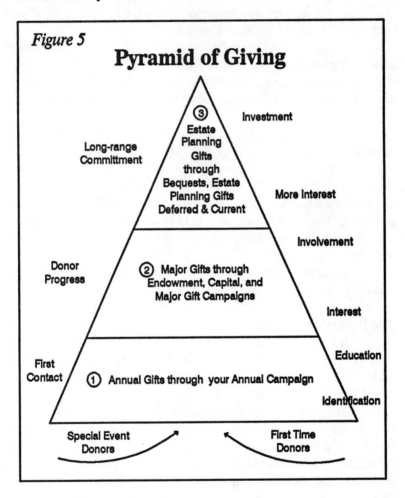

Figure 5

Pyramid of Giving

③ Investment

Estate Planning Gifts through Bequests, Estate Planning Gifts Deferred & Current

Long-range Committment

More Interest

Involvement

Donor Progress

② Major Gifts through Endowment, Capital, and Major Gift Campaigns

Interest

Education

First Contact

① Annual Gifts through your Annual Campaign

Identification

Special Event Donors

First Time Donors

The Cultivation of Donors

What is the fallout rate of interim givers? 20%
How many new donors will you need to grow? 21%

Fund Raising 101

Chapter Six

Organizational Writing

Organizational writing is important because it is used in so many different ways to promote and explain your charity. If you haven't started yet, I recommend that you begin your organizational writing with a mission statement.

An effective mission statement defines the fundamental and unique purposes that sets your institution apart from the other institutions of its type, and it identifies the scope of the institution's operations. There are eight **components** that can be used to make an effective mission statement:

1. Identification of target customer base
2. Identification of principal product or service
3. Area served
4. Core technologies
5. An expression of commitment to survival, growth, and profitability
6. Key elements in the organization's philosophy
7. Organization's self-concept
8. Organization's desired self-image

It's not necessary for all eight to be in a mission statement for it to be effective. You can use as many of the components as is necessary to accurately reflect your charity's mission.

Reasons for a Mission or Case Statement

There are various reasons for a mission statement. The two that first come to mind are (1) helping to make decisions and take actions that are consistent with accomplishing the mission of the institution, and (2) helping to define and communicate the institution's role to the public so as to establish responsibility and accountability by all those with responsibility.

To develop a mission statement, invite all those individuals who share responsibility for the institution to participate. Encourage input from everyone as to what the institution's mission should be. Each participant can write a preliminary statement.

Next, list all input received on a blackboard or a flip chart. A discussion leader should encourage exchange. Record all the items that the separate mission statements have in common. Be sure to point out and discuss the various strengths of each participant's statement.

When you have completed your work, you could end up with all eight components in your statement. Even if you don't, you should have discussed the importance of identifying your constituency, the principal service or product that you have to offer, the geographic area that you serve, any technology or service that is uniquely yours, an expression of commitment to survival, growth, and profitability, your organization's philosophy, your organization's concept of itself, and how you wish the public to see your organization.

Although including all eight components in your mission statement is optional, the minimum mission statement should include why the institution exists and what your primary goal is.

Following are three examples of a mission statement:

1. We believe animal rights to be the worthiest of goals and we will work until Congress passes HB #284.

2.   We are dedicated to creating the finest quality products and will deliver them at the most reasonable prices.

3.   We want to ensure that flower lovers receive the highest quality roses found anywhere

An example of a mission statement for a center for handicapped adults might read as follows:

We want to provide the environment through which physically handicapped adults can acquire the ability to live independently.

As you can see, many of the components are left out of this example. Why? Because they would not have added anything of value, and they would have made the mission statement more difficult to memorize. Although memorization is not necessary, a mission statement will be more useful if it is easy to read and understand and can be committed easily to memory.

Case Statements

A case statement is one of the most important pieces in the fund-raising effort. It should be as compelling as possible. You will use it to convince individuals, businesses, or foundations that you are worthy and deserving of their support. In short, it should be as powerful as the Gettysburg Address.

There is a logical set of steps you can go through to arrive at a compelling case statement. We cover these eight steps below:

1.   The institution's mission statement should be worked into the first or second sentence of the case statement.

The mission of the Adult Handicapped Center is to provide an environment through which physically handicapped adults acquire the ability to live independently.

2.   The next few sentences should include a brief history and an outline of the track record of the institution. Be sure to tell why it can be relied on to solve the problem.

For more than twenty years, the Adult Handicapped Center has provided the necessary support to assist young adults in getting the start they need.

3.   Give details of major organizational goals, strategies, and specific objectives related to each goal.

> *Without the Adult Handicapped Center, there would be no opportunity for handicapped adults to learn urgently needed skills for independent living.*

4.   Outline the assets the institution has to apply toward the solution of the problem—facilities, staff and other professional resources, volunteer manpower, and so forth.

> *The Adult Handicapped Center has assembled most of the necessary equipment and has developed an expert staff trained to meet the needs of these exceptional people.*

5.   Provide evidence of management competency and financial accountability, including the most recently audited financial statements.

> *On duty at all times are a resident manager, who has a master's degree in environmental psychology, and two physical therapists.*

6.   Include an accurate depiction of the problems the institution will address and the people affected.

> *The Center, with your help, will continue to provide local handicapped individuals with the training and support that are not available anywhere else within 100 miles.*

7.   Describe demographic, socio-economic, and other data that could be useful to the donor.

> *No individual is excluded because of age, sex, color, religion, or inability to pay.*

8.   Address relevant future and long-range goals of the organization to provide greater services to have a further impact on the problem.

> *The handicapped individuals of Northeast Tennessee had no place like the Adult Handicapped Center for many years. It is the commitment of the board that the area will never again be without these valuable services.*

Organizational Writing

The following case statement shows how these eight parts read when they are put together as a unit.

The Case for the Adult Handicapped Center

The mission of the Adult Handicapped Center is to provide the environment through which physically handicapped adults acquire the ability to live independently.

For more than twenty years, the Adult Handicapped Center has provided the necessary support to assist young adults in getting the start they needed. Without the Adult Handicapped Center, there would be no opportunity for handicapped adults to learn urgently needed independent living skills.

The Adult Handicapped Center has assembled most of the necessary equipment and has developed an expert staff trained to meet these exceptional people's needs. On duty at all times are a resident manager, who has a master's degree in environmental psychology, and two physical therapists.

The Center, with your help, will continue to provide adult handicapped individuals with the training and support that are not available anywhere else within 100 miles. No individual is excluded due to age, sex, color, religion, or their ability to pay. The handicapped individuals of Northeast Tennessee had no place like the Adult Handicapped Center for many years. It is the commitment of the board that the area will never again be without these valuable services.

Although the Adult Handicapped Center is a mythical organization, I think you can see that with a little work the eight parts of a case statement can be made to read very smoothly and will produce a compelling argument for financial support.

Additional Information on Case Statements

Most professional fund raisers agree that, if a case statement is both short and compelling, it is more effective. However, there may be times, or there may be areas of the country, where a two- to three-page case statement is called for, and on rare occasions you may need to have a case statement of ten to fifteen pages.

You will know when a longer case statement is necessary. For instance, if you can't tell the story in one page, then by all means, take two or more. However, I know from experience that unless persons reading the case have a personal investment in your institution, they are not likely to want to read much about it.

Be on the Winning Team

Have you ever noticed how the stands of a baseball stadium fill up when the team is winning? You can't get a ticket at any price. When the team is losing, you can't give your ticket away. People are like that when it comes to supporting a charity. It is human nature to want to be on the side of the winner. Make sure that your case statement represents your charity as being successful.

For more than twenty years, the Adult Handicapped Center has provided the necessary support needed to assist young adults in getting the start they need.

For more than twenty years illustrates that your charity has been around for a while and has *provided the necessary support to assist young adults in getting the start they need*, illustrates that even further.

People Give for Different Reasons

I'm certain you realize that people give for different reasons. If you want to ensure success with your written documents, you need to know what the concerns are for the target audience and write accordingly. For example:

Without the Adult Handicapped Center, there would be no opportunity for handicapped adults to learn independent living skills.

If you are writing to an audience that is known for having compassion for other people's problems, you will have above-average success with this message. For example, women over sixty years of age would be a target audience for a message of this nature.

Organizational Writing

If you are preparing to write a letter to people who you know are anti-KKK, would you want to use illustrations in your message that talked about how KKK members deserve their individual rights? NO!

A Good Investment

Donors want to know how their money will help solve the charity's problem. You should start by identifying the problem, then focus on how the success of your project will aid in solving that problem, and assure your prospects that by contributing they too will be helping with the solution.

An upper-body motor skills machine (a T-bol-lee) is badly needed. We have identified the problem to be a badly needed T-bol-lee. Now we want to tell how the problem will be solved if our project succeeds. *With the T-bol-lee the residents will be able to build upper-body strength and increase their opportunities for employment as well as being able to do more for themselves.* This last sentence is intended to encourage prospects to feel that they will not be alone in their support: there will be many others. *Won't you join with the hundreds of others who have given so generously?*

Persuade to Act

We have tried to be compelling in what we have written. Whatever you do, don't lose sight of the fact that the purpose of your case statement is to persuade prospects to act in the form of a monetary response.

Mr. Doyle, your gift of $500 will make the dream come true.

(A T-bol-lee is an imaginary piece of machinery invented to be used in this example only.)

Proposal Writing

Another example of organizational writing is the proposal. Proposals are most often used in grant writing and capital campaigning. However, many fund raisers have discovered that a well-written and well-documented proposal improves their chances for a cash gift. Therefore, if the support they are seeking is important to them, more often than not, they will take the time to create a written proposal.

Information a Proposal Should Contain

It is commonly believed that a proposal can be as short as one or two pages. However, it is generally held that a proposal can be up to ten pages and have another ten pages of backup materials. I have never allowed myself more than ten pages and feel comfortable in recommending the same for you. I also include backup materials up to ten pages, and it is very important that these materials have an index page showing where to find a specific detail.

The following is a logical sequence of a written proposal:

A Title Page - A Proposal for the Adult Handicapped Center. (This page could also have the name of the prospect who is being called upon for the gift. And many times this page will also include the amount of financial support being asked for.)

Project Description - Statement of the case followed by how the money will be spent. Also, list the methods that will be used to gain visibility for the donor.

Table of Contents - Carefully arrange each piece of backup material to be used.
- Includes a copy of the 501(c)(3) federal tax exemption.
- Give a brief history of your institution.
- Provide a realistic budget.
- List the volunteer leadership (officers and board with full names, companies, and mailing addresses).
- List any experts who will be associated with the grant (one-page resumes would be in order).

Organizational Writing

-- Outline previous successes (newspaper and magazine articles are recommended).
-- Supply letters from individuals who have benefitted from previous programs.

We have covered the three most important pieces of organizational writing in this chapter. You will have many opportunities to use the third one, and because of its importance, we will delve deeper into proposal writing in Chapter 17.

Fund Raising 101

Chapter Seven

Planning and Financial Reports

Many fund raisers are fearful of financial reports. Don't be. In this chapter we talk about and show examples of financial reports. If you already have financial reports that work for you, then you don't need to try to make them look like these. All I hope to accomplish is to show several examples and explain why and how to use them.

The purpose of some of the financial reports that I've included are to aid you in the planning process. Others are to assist you in reporting results to your volunteer leadership and anyone else who needs to know.

I again use the fictional Adult Handicapped Center as the charity for which we are creating financial records. The examples in this chapter include an annual organizational plan, a five-year organization plan, a budget, a revenue comparison statement, and a financial plan. With these five financial statements, you will know as much as you need to know to do a good job.

A Long-Range Plan

Any long-range plan for five or more years is the responsibility of your volunteer leadership. A long-range plan

65

developed by your volunteers will tell everyone where it is they want to go. That's not to say that they must sit down and write it, but it should reflect their goals and aspirations in accomplishing your organization's mission. In fact, you will likely be the author of the first draft, and then with your input, the plan will be altered to its final form. I must warn you, however, that if the board doesn't feel ownership in your long-range goals, you are going to have to win their support over and over.

The purpose of a five-year plan is to allow you and your volunteer leadership the opportunity to set goals and objectives designed to lead toward the accomplishment of your mission. The five-year plan commits everyone for the long haul. Two quick examples: a mail program requires five to ten years to mature and a planned giving program even longer, ten to twenty years. You can see that a five- or ten-year plan allows you and your volunteers to make the kind of commitment that will be necessary to accomplish a measure of maturity in either of those two programs.

The five-year plan is surprisingly simple and has very little detail, being just detailed enough to keep you pointed in the right direction. Remember, your executive committee can change the five-year plan any time they feel the target is no longer accurate. Although the executive director can't change it on her or his own, the director certainly has the right and obligation to point out changes that would more accurately reflect where the organization wants to go.

In a way, a five-year plan is similar to the mission statement. It's the first financial record you work on, and like the mission statement, everything concerning your finances builds on it. (See Figure 6 for a sample five year plan.)

Planning and Financial Reports

Figure 6

THE ADULT HANDICAPPED CENTER

FIVE-YEAR GOAL: July 1986-1991
Updated and Revised Annually

1.   Center to raise $1 million in cash gifts and planned giving sources by 6/91.

2.   Interest from reserve and endowment funds shall grow to a level that is sufficient to offset 50 percent of the operating cost of the Center.

3.   Development Office to distribute funds to the Center for use in operations.

4.   Center fund-raising activities are as follows:

    A. Current Giving — Special Events
        Walk-a-thon
        Black-Tie Dinner
        Scavenger Hunt
        Direct Mail

    B. Rental Income, HUD Subsidy, & Tenant Supplement

    C. Major Gift Planning:
        a. Current Gifts
        b. Deferred Gifts
            ..   Trusts
            -   Pooled Income Funds
            ..   Annuities
        c. Capital Campaign

5.   Center will maintain a well-rounded recognition program for all types of giving.

    A. Donors
    B. Volunteers
    C. Staff

The annual and five-year plans are not documents that you will refer to daily. I don't mean to lessen their importance; it's just that once you have the general direction planted in your and your volunteers' memories, you won't need to refer to the plans very often. The budget is the financial report that you will use more often.

Fund Raising 101

An Annual Organization Plan

The purpose of the annual organizational plan is to provide you and your volunteer leadership the opportunity to set goals and objectives concerning what you intend to do in the area of development.

It is always helpful in planning if you can evaluate the results of last year before or as you construct the annual plan. It's even more helpful if you have several years to evaluate. We are going to assume some things for our example, and we will come back to evaluation later.

Our first assumption is that we will be planning on a fiscal year, July 1, 1993, to June 30, 1994. Under fund-raising goals, the first is to raise $454,000, using annual support, rental income, investment income, planned giving, and memorials. Notice that these categories are broad; we will be more specific later in other reports.

Second, we show that we expect to conduct a walk, a black-tie dinner, a scavenger hunt, and a mail program. Rental income is also broken down to show where it comes from, although the amounts are not specified.

Planned giving is broken into a separate category because we are assuming that it is a stand-alone department. It can be included with the other income sources.

Another projection that is usually included in an organization plan is some statement addressing donor growth. We have indicated a 20 percent growth from 2,200 donors to 2,640 donors during the year. That's important because if we are to continue to show financial growth in our organization, we need new donors.

The rest of the organization plan addresses specific office management objectives and recognition objectives. You may wish to include other goals and objectives in your annual organizational plan. Don't try to be exact in your projections. Just try to create a target that you and your volunteer leadership can shoot for. And, if you remember from earlier chapters, this in one of the things that you and the finance committee draft and the executive committee either approves or not. Once it is approved, you can move forward with other financial reports.

Some fund raisers believe that the annual plan is drawn up entirely by the development officer without input from volunteers, and that the development officer then executes the plan. I have no quarrel with this philosophy; it's just that I have never had volunteers who would follow me very far without having input into where we would go and how we would get there. Make a rough draft of your annual plan, and deliver it to the development committee for their input or blessing before making it final. (See Figure 7 for a sample annual plan.)

The Annual Budget

The purpose of an annual budget is to provide you and your volunteers with the specific details concerning the projections of revenue and expenses. The budget in the example is what I would refer to as a simple budget. Every revenue source has a separate line item, as do the expense items. There is no necessity to lay it out the way that I have. You may vary yours as you wish.

The revenue line items consist of the annual fund drive, the direct mail programs, corporate gifts, foundation gifts, and so on. I always separate planned giving, memorials, and other programs. You can leave them the way I'm showing you, or you can include them as another line item along with the other revenue sources. I like showing them this way because I feel that it gives them greater emphasis. Investments are linked to the economy, and rental income depends on occupancy and rates.

You will notice that there are two columns, budget and actual. The budget is what you projected as revenue for this year, and the actual is what actually came in during the year. When scanning the budget, you can see at a glance if you are projecting an increase in next year's budget. If you are the author of these numbers, your volunteers may ask you to defend them. If the volunteers are involved in the drafting of the numbers, they will need

Fund Raising 101

Figure 7   THE ADULT HANDICAPPED CENTER
ANNUAL PLAN
FY 1993/94 Objectives:

Fund-Raising Goals:

1. By June 30, 1993, to raise in cash $454,000 through:

A.	Annual Support	$250,000
B.	Rental Income	175,000
C.	Investment Income	5,000
D.	Planned Giving	20,000
E.	Memorials	4,000
	TOTAL	$454,000

2. Current Support:
    A. Walk-a-thon, Black-Tie Dinner, Scavenger Hunt, Mail
    B. Rental Income, HUD, Subsidy, & Tenant Supplement
    C. Interest from $102,000
    D. Gifts from honorariums and memorials

3. Planned Giving: (current giving, deferred giving and capital campaign)
    A. Wills and Bequests
    B. Work on Major Gifts Committee prospects
    C. Continue to cultivate and mail Planned Giving Newsletter
    D. Conduct Appreciation Event
    E. Continue with educational programs and visits to the Center

4. To maintain current donor base and grow by 20 percent.

FY 1992/93	FY 1993/94
2,200	2,640

Office Management

1. To employ and train new, as well as current, employees to maintain present fund-raising programs and to institute new programs if necessary to meet FY 1993/94 revenue goals.
2. Continue to enhance computer capabilities to handle an increasing donor base.
3. Continue to train and cross-train staff in administrative responsibilities of the development office in order to be prepared as needs arise.
4. Continue to improve computer system to appropriately recognize and thank every gift to the Center.
5. Continue to evaluate accounting needs in an effort to become proficient with our accounting system.

Recognition

1. Continue to see that all major and endowment gifts are recognized.
2. Continue the recognition effort for all other forms of giving.
3. Send thank-you letters and certificates to all volunteers who work on the fund-raising events and on any other event when warranted.
4. Consider an open house or reception when appropriate (for example, for employees who worked on fund raisers).

less selling. You can see that the budgeted $454,000 in revenue is greater than the actual revenue for last year of $422,538.

The expenses usually follow on the lower half of the page or the second page if necessary. I have listed eighteen line items alphabetically. You may wish to use fewer than eighteen, or you may want to use more. Use whatever you and your volunteers feel most at ease with. It is important for you to be realistic in your projections. It would be unusual for next year's expense budget to be less than the prior year. However, with everyone in the country cutting back to gain a competitive edge, it might be necessary to cut back on expenses.

The nonoperating expenses usually have something to do with depreciation. Again, take advice from a CPA who is on your board on matters of this type.

If you remember from the chapter on committees, you should be recruiting help from your CPAs and other members of the finance committee. After you and the finance committee have drafted a document that everyone feels is realistic, then together you are ready to present your recommendations to the executive committee for approval. (See Figure 8 for sample budget.)

The Revenue and Expense Statement

The revenue and expense statement provides you and your volunteers with a financial report system that will keep all of you informed about where you are with your income from fund raising and what you are spending to raise those funds. The revenue comparison statement in the example is fairly straightforward in its presentation. Every income source is a separate line item and so are the expense items. And once again, there is no magic in laying it out the way that I have. You may vary as you wish. The revenue line items consist of the annual fund drive, the direct mail programs, corporate gifts, foundation gifts, and so on. I have separated planned giving, memorials, and other programs for emphasis. You can leave them the way I've laid them out, or you can just include them as another line item along with the other revenue sources. Investments

Fund Raising 101

Figure 8   THE ADULT HANDICAPPED CENTER
FY 1993/94 Sample Budget

REVENUE		93/94	92/93
ANNUAL FUND DRIVE		Budget	Actual
Direct Mail Programs		$ 28,000	$ 25,245
Corporate Gifts		15,000	12,000
Foundation Gifts		5,000	5,000
Leadership Gifts		100,000	89,500
Support Groups		4,000	4,500
Special Events Held		94,000	82,985
TOTAL FUND-RAISING		$250,000	$219,230
Planned Gifts Received	20,000	18,000	
Memorials		4,000	4,255
OTHER PROGRAMS			
-Investments		5,000	5,213
-Rental		175,000	175,840
TOTAL INCOME		$454,000	$422,538
EXPENSES			
Ads and Promotions	1,000	850	
Donor Recognition		2,500	2,113
Employee Compensation		26,000	22,400
Employee Benefits		5,200	5,368
Forms & Printing		10,500	10,135
Fund-Raising Specials	1,000	1,072	
Insurance		1,000	950
Maintenance Contracts	600	500	
Meetings		1,200	1,154
Miscellaneous		1,000	718
Office Supplies		6,000	5,821
Postage		12,000	11,198
Professional Development		4,000	3,800
Professional Fees		3,000	2,500
Publications		350	297
Rental and Lease Expense		12,000	12,000
Telethon		1,500	1,879
Travel & Lodging		800	659
TOTAL EXPENSE		$ 89,650	$ 83,414
Total Nonoperating			
Expenses		5,000	4,379
TOTAL EXPENSES		$ 94,650	$ 87,793
NET INCOME		$359,350	$334,745

are linked to the economy, and rental income depends on occupancy and rates.

When planning your revenue and expense statement for the entire year, you have to make some assumptions. Once again, having the history of prior years can help you considerably. Under current year, show actual costs (what you actually brought into your office during this month) and the budget (what you budgeted to come in during this month). If you budgeted $500 in the annual fund line item and you brought in only $450, you may not need to get too excited. It may be that you budgeted $500 the next month and you bring in $600. These minor differences can often be attributed to timing errors.

It is another matter if you consistently under-perform in a revenue line item or overspend in an expense line item. If you see this becoming a trend over three or four months, you and your volunteers may wish to alter your revenue and expense statement. It could be that there is a very good reason for the problem; altering the statement would make sense. (See Figure 9 for a sample revenue and expense statement.)

The Financial Plan

The financial plan is the last financial statement we deal with in this chapter. The purpose of the financial plan is to get down to specifics on the source of the revenue and how it will be coming into your office. Actually break down each category of revenue from your revenue and expense statement. Under annual giving, break down direct mail into each mailing in each category that you mail. Estimate the number of gifts that you expect to receive and what the average dollar amount for each gift will be. Do the same in each category--corporate gifts, foundation gifts, and the like.

When you have finished with your financial plan, estimate the total number of gifts that you expect to receive and the average gift size for each category. It's not hard to know what your job is if you have this information. Also, it's not hard to evaluate

Fund Raising 101

Figure 9

The Adult Handicapped Center
FY 1993/94 Revenue and Expense Statement

REVENUE

	Current Month Actual	Current Month Budget	Year to Date Actual	Year to Date Budget
Annual Fund Drive				
Direct Mail Programs	$ 455	$ 500	29,172	28,000
Corporate Gifts	1,125	1,500	15,000	15,000
Foundation Gifts	0	0	5,000	5,000
Leadership Gifts	2,000	1,000	101,025	100,000
Support Groups	500	0	4,214	4,000
Special Events Held	$18,235	$12,000	$ 99,630	$ 98,000
TOTAL FUND-RAISING	$22,315	15,000	254,041	250,000
Planned Gifts Received	0	1,500	17,500	20,000
Memorials	200	300	4,000	4,000
OTHER PROGRAMS				
-Investments	1,122	500	10,250	5,000
-Rental	$ 1,520	$ 1,450	173,544	175,000
TOTAL INCOME	$15,157	$19,250	459,335	454,000

EXPENSES

	Current Month Actual	Current Month Budget	Year to Date Actual	Year to Date Budget
Ads and Promotions	0	860	1,000	
Donor Recognition	25	200	3,100	2,500
Employee Compensation	2,150	2,166	25,890	26,000
Employee Benefits	421	433	5,119	5,200
Forms & Printing	1,120	800	10,575	10,500
Fund-Raise Special	0	50	650	1,000
Insurance	0	0	990	1,000
Maintenance Contracts	0	600	600	
Meetings	95	100	1,435	1,200
Miscellaneous	35	50	987	1,000
Office Supplies	755	500	7,006	6,000
Postage	68	100	11,109	12,000
Professional Development	0	0	2,910	4,000
Professional Fees	0	0	3,300	3,000
Publications	0	0	328	350
Rental and Lease Expense	1,000	1,000	12,000	12,000
Telethon	236	200	1,155	1,500
Travel and Lodging	105	100	723	800
SUB TOTAL	6,010	5,599	$88,737	$89,650
Total Nonoperating Expenses	4,785	5,000	$ 4,785	$ 5,000
TOTAL EXPENSES	$ 10,795	$ 10,599	$ 93,522	$94,650
NET INCOME	$ 4,362	$ 8,651	$365,813	$359,350

Planning and Financial Reports

Figure 10 **The Financial Plan** to Obtain Resources
(Working backward from annual budget, considering all potential sources.)

	No. of Gifts	Gift History: Prior Year Gift Income	Fund Raise Budgeted	FR Actual Cost	% cost to $s raised
FOR 92/93					
ANNUAL FUND DRIVE					
Direct Mail Programs					
-Prospect Mail #1	650	5,500	4,300	4,350	0.96
-Direct Mail #1	421	12,000	175	210	0.02
-Prospect Mail #2	550	3,300	3,300	3,500	1.06
-Direct Mail #2	220	7,200	175	200	0.04
Corporate Gifts	3	15,000	2,000	920	0.06
Foundation Gifts	1	5,000	1,250	550	0.11
LEADERSHIP GIFTS					
-Board Trustees	24	6,725	1,000	300	0.04
-Staff Gifts	9	3,675	250	50	0.01
-Major Gifts	20	89,600	5,000	10,900	0.12
SUPPORT GROUPS					
-Civic Clubs	29	2,475	100	0	0.00
-Churches	11	1,275	100	0	0.00
-Mothers Clubs	4	250	50	0	0.00
SPECIAL EVENTS HELD					
-Walk-a-thon (30)	600	3,234	1,000	626	0.20
-County Walks (22)	400	2,140	1,000	402	0.20
-Black-Tie Auction(290)	780	59,123	15,000	8,763	0.15
-Pit Party (1,143)	320	10,050	5,000	3,025	0.26
-Scavenger Hunt (32)	590	15,125	4,000	4,790	0.32
-Handicapped Drive	241	8,328	3,000	2,952	0.35
Memorials	160	4,000	4,000	0	0
Planned Gifts Received	3	20,000	10,000	6,295	0.46
TOTAL FUND-RAISING	5,036	274,000	56,700	47,833	0.18
OTHER PROGRAMS:					
-Investments	--	5,000	275	270	0.10
-Rental	--	$175,000			
TOTAL REVENUE		$454,000			

whether or not you are doing a good job with this type of information. (See Figure 10 for a sample financial plan.)

You can spend the rest of your life creating one financial plan after another. Sooner or later you will have to get down to the business of fund raising. With these five financial plans, you can answer 99.9 percent of the questions that you will be asked about your plans for your organization's revenue and expenses.

Chapter Eight

How You Ask Makes The Difference

I discovered long ago that volunteers are considerably more willing to make calls on potential donors if they feel that they know what to say. If you can add motivation, you have a powerful volunteer. In my mind, that means that I must teach volunteers what to say and then properly motivate them so that they want to go out and ask for the gift.

As you already know, it's a lot easier to say these things than actually to do them. However, I have been very lucky in training and motivating most of the volunteers that I've worked with. I am certain that one of the reasons I've been able to teach and inspire volunteers is that I have truly believed in the importance of the charities I've served.

In training volunteers, I have used a ten-step approach that I call "How You Ask Makes The Difference." I like this approach so much that I have developed a video of the entire process. I have used these steps over the years to train hundreds of volunteers and fund-raising professionals. More than $30 million has been raised using these steps.

If you will learn these steps and teach them to your volunteers, I'm sure you will find "How You Ask Makes The Difference" to be very helpful!

The purpose of this chapter is to acquaint volunteers and professionals alike with the steps in asking a prospect for financial support. The techniques suggested are tried and true, having been tested over many years. However, it is not uncommon for people who use the ten steps to vary slightly in order to include their own personalities. In fact, I encourage everyone to use the steps in a way that feels comfortable to them.

Once you and your volunteers have learned the ten steps, all of you will be able to call upon a broad cross section of support from foundations, large corporations, small businesses, and wealthy individuals.

There are many tenets with which a fund raiser should be familiar, but there are only two of what I call commandments, and they are:

"People do not give until they are asked,"
and
"Calling on people face-to-face is the most effective method of solicitation."

Like anything else you learn, techniques alone cannot ensure your success. The most critical element in any solicitation is the person making the call. In solicitation of donors, I sometimes refer to the four Ms. You:

MUST be enthusiastic about what you are doing.
MUST understand the cause.
MUST be determined that the goal will be met.
MUST be persistent in your follow-up.

If the volunteers making the solicitation call have all four of these MUSTS, the chances are many times greater that they will receive the financial support being sought.

As in any successful business, volunteers calling on prospects in behalf of charities follow a logical set of steps. The ten that I use are as follows:

1. **Prepare for the visit.**
2. **Know as much as you can about your prospects.**
3. **Make an appointment.**
4. **Visit your prospect.**
5. **Share your reason for being there.**
6. **Ask for the gift.**
7. **Know how to handle objections.**
8. **Be persistent with follow-up.**
9. **Write a thank-you note.**
10. **Stay in touch and turn in your paperwork.**

Let's review the ten steps one at a time.

Step 1 -- Prepare for the Visit
Begin preparing for the visit by taking advantage of any how-to training that is being offered by the soliciting charity.

Also, in preparing for the visit you must be informed.

-        Familiarize yourself with any materials available such as the case statement for support, brochures about the charity, newspaper articles, and such. Decide where to go for answers that you do not have. Know how your fund-raising committee fits into the overall scheme of the organization. Know if there are benefits that can be offered to the prospect such as Giving Clubs or Recognition Dinners.

If you are **NOT** reluctant to make calls, you are probably in the minority when it comes to asking for money. Few people if any are really completely comfortable about asking other people for money. However, this reluctance can be used to your advantage. The persons on whom you will be calling on dislike being in your place as much as you do. They have likely made solicitation calls themselves and they are sympathetic to your situation. There are only two things that will cause your prospect to lose respect for you: being ill-prepared and being insincere.

STEP 2 -- Know As Much As You Can About Your Prospects

When I say, "Know as much as you can about your prospect," I don't mean that you have to be acquainted with the prospect. In fact, some people feel better when calling on complete strangers. I know I do. What I really mean is that anything and everything that you can learn about the prospect's involvement with the charity can be helpful to the volunteer who makes the call. The more your volunteers know about the prospects they are calling on, the better their chances are of receiving the support that they will be requesting. The organization staff should prepare a brief report on each of the prospects that the volunteers have agreed to ask for support.

Volunteers need to know the prospects'
* giving history, including last gift amount;
* any known complaints by the prospects about the organization;
* any previous association with the organization.

If there were any problems, the volunteers should be informed and should address them first, being sure to thank the prospect for previous support. After the problem has been addressed, the volunteer is free to move on to the next step.

Step 3 -- Make an Appointment

Even before making the first appointment, volunteers should make their own gifts. By doing so, volunteers demonstrate their sincerity and commitment, and it will give them confidence as they begin making their calls.

Next, volunteers should pick the prospects with whom they are most likely to succeed. Volunteers should telephone those prospects and indicate their willingness to be flexible about the time and the meeting place. *Strongly resist discussing the gift on the phone.* There is really no substitute for face-to-face visits. Over the years, fund raisers have found telephone solicitation to

How You Ask Makes the Difference

be a very poor second choice and writing to the prospects to be even worse.

Let me reiterate: **RESIST** discussing the gift by phone. If the prospect is persistent, the volunteer can say, *"Mr. Jones, we value your opinion and talking with you in person is very important to me."*

Sometimes, no matter how hard you try, the prospect will not make an appointment. Don't worry; it happens to everyone. Go on to the next prospect. You may have heard of the rule of thirds. There are several definitions of the rule of thirds; I have personally heard of three or four. The one I am referring to is that one third of the prospects give what you ask for or more, one third give less than they are asked for, and the final third give nothing at all.

I wish it were that simple. I have experienced 100 percent giving; although it was a small group, it does happen. And I have experienced many other percentages. One thing is certain. Your percentages of givers increases if you are true to the seven logical steps in donor cultivation that we covered in Chapter 5.

Once you have the appointment with a prospect, you've taken a giant step.

Step 4 -- Visit Your Prospect

There is considerable difference of opinion on the next step. Some of our better-known and successful fund-raising professionals believe that a good deal of small talk is helpful when making a solicitation call. I do not feel that a great deal of small talk is good. If you teach your volunteers that small talk is good, then you have to be particularly careful to recruit volunteers who are adept at this art.

I firmly believe that over 90 percent of the prospects on whom your volunteers call will want them to get to the point and get out. Understand that I don't mean that a volunteer should be abrupt or rude. I usually start by saying, *"Thank you, Mr. Jones for working me into your busy schedule. I realize that time is money, so if you don't mind I'll explain why I'm here to see you today."*

Fund Raising 101

Some small talk can put the prospects at ease, but try to keep it brief. Prospects know or suspect why your volunteers are there and will appreciate their keeping the visit as short as possible. You can usually encourage a positive interview by starting out with a statement similar to: *"Mr. Jones, I wanted to call on you because I value your opinion, and you have always been generous about supporting important community projects."*

Step 5 -- Share Your Reason for Being There

If your volunteers have been trained properly and if they have done their homework, they now have an opportunity to use it. After small talk they can:

- Move to the organization's role in the community.
- Tell about recent programs the charity has conducted.
- Cover the specific needs that will be paid for by the campaign.
- Tell why they felt compelled to get involved.
- Mention that they have already made a commitment.
- Wind up with how the prospect and the prospect's family will benefit from the results of the improvements made to the charity.

Step 6 -- Ask for the Gift

Remember, there is more than one approach. We will cover the following two:

1. If the prospect is in fact a previous donor.
2. If the prospect is being asked for the first time.

To a previous donor the volunteer might say: *"Mr. Jones, I want to thank you again for your previous support. For this campaign, we are hoping you will consider a gift in the range of $2,000 a year, for the next five years. If this amount is too low, that would be great. If this amount is too high, please feel free to give whatever is comfortable for you and your family at this time".*

How You Ask Makes the Difference

At this point, the volunteer has done all he or she can do, and silence is in order. If the volunteer continues to talk, it is very possible that all the good that has been done could be undone.

If this is a new prospect, the volunteer might try the following: *"Mr. Jones, businesses similar to yours are being asked to consider a gift in the range of $2,000 a year for the next five years. Naturally, we will be happy to have your support at whatever level is comfortable for you and your family at this time."*

Allow the prospect to react or comment **and listen** to what he says. Often, we are so tense that we fail to hear something important the prospect is telling us.

When Finished -- It's Time to Be Silent

In fact, salesmen will tell you that the skill of selective deafness is very important. A good salesman is deaf to "NO" and understands that "no" frequently precedes "yes."

Treat "NO" responses as follows: *"Perhaps we asked at the wrong time. When would be better?"* or, *"Is there something that we can do that would make it easier to say yes?"*

The volunteer can respond to a firm and final "no" with, *"Let me give you time to think it over, and I'll get back to you soon."*

Step 7 -- Know How to Handle Objections

If you are listening, you will hear objections. How you handle them is very important. Many successful salesmen repeat the objection to indicate that they understand. It is important to avoid an argumentative attitude and to address the objection positively.

Prospect: *"We gave to the capital campaign, I don't think we want to give again now."*

Solicitor: *"Yes, I am aware that you contributed to the capital campaign and very generously. Many of us did, and our support played a major role in the improvements that have taken*

83

place over the last five years. You and I, our families, and all our friends and neighbors have benefitted by our sacrifices. I think you can agree that the need for this fine organization continues. In light of the great ABC program, your support is no less important today, than it was five years ago. I am continuing my support. I hope you understand why I am once again asking you to consider a gift in the range of $2,000 a year for the next five years."

Before leaving, if appropriate, ask the prospect for names of any friends or relatives on whom you should call for a gift.

The Finishing Touch

Many prospects can and will make a decision on the first visit. However, if the volunteer is unable to obtain a commitment on the first call, be sure to ask for a specific time to return, by saying something like: *"Mr. Jones, I believe what I am doing to help this organization is important, but like you, time is money to me, and I need to make a living. Can I count on you to give me an answer by next Monday or Tuesday?"*

Step 8 -- Be Persistent With Follow-Up

Maybe the hardest part in soliciting in behalf of any charity is being persistent until the prospect answers yes or no. However, all the work to this point will have gone for naught if the volunteer doesn't continue to follow up until a conclusion is determined.

Step 9 - Write a Thank-You Note

It is strongly recommended that the volunteer solicitor take the time to send a short hand-written note thanking the prospect for the gift, or the time if that is all that has been given.

Step 10 - Stay in Touch and Turn in Your Paperwork

Keeping the charity's staff apprised of the progress helps to eliminate confusion, keeps the other interested parties informed, and goes a long way in helping to eliminate anxiety among all concerned. And finally, give the charity any information concerning the prospect.

Additional Thoughts

Ask your volunteers to be sure to make written notes of the visit. Their experiences can be helpful to the person who makes the next call.

The staff and the volunteers of the charity make up a team. The staff exists to provide continuity and assistance to the volunteers. The volunteers give as much of their time and expertise as possible in order to keep cost to a minimum, thus providing greater benefit to the cause both groups serve. The volunteers should be encouraged to ask for help or answers to their questions.

Don't allow the volunteers to get discouraged if they are not successful their first time out. And remember, the very best baseball players rarely hit much over .300; that's only three hits out of ten times at bat. Your volunteers' average will be determined by several things, such as technique and attitude, which were mentioned earlier. Volunteers should choose people over whom they may have influence. Also, keep in mind: have the right person asking for the right gift at the right time. That's a winning combination.

Your volunteers may not bat a thousand, but every call they make increases the awareness of your charity in the community. They demonstrate the quality of leadership that supports your charity, and at the same time, pave the way for a future gift.

I have the philosophy that people who do not give to a particular cause generally fall into only one category. They do not see the value in their sacrifice for themselves, their family, or their business. If they did, they might be asking you!

Motives for Giving

Sometimes, people are motivated to give for reasons other than the fact that a volunteer calls on them. Some of the strongest motivations that cause individuals or businesses to lend support include, but are not limited to, the following:

Fund Raising 101

☞ They are being asked by someone they know and respect.
☞ They owe a favor to the person doing the solicitation.
☞ They are seeking visibility and recognition for themselves ᴏ their company.
☞ They are in sympathy with the mission of the charity.

Some of the less strong motives include:
- They have a sense of obligation.
- There are tax benefits from making the gift.
- They are embarrassed or feel guilty if they do not give.

You should be able to name others. There are probably as many motivations for people to contribute to one charity or another as there are people. The more successful fund raisers, whether volunteer or professional, learn how to identify an individual's motivation and use it in their presentation.

Other motives include enjoying power, having a strong ego, having need to belong, wishing to demonstrate a point, and so on. As you can plainly see, there are many motives for making a gift.

Be Where the Donors Are When They Want to Give

Do you recall the national Statue of Liberty Campaign of a few years ago? I wanted to contribute; I was waiting only for the right opportunity. My opportunity finally came in the Sunday newspaper in the form of an advertisement in <u>Parade Magazine</u>. The advertisement gave the address to which I could send a contribution. For a contribution of $1 to $9, I could receive a bronze-colored plastic pin. For $10 or more, I could have a silver-colored plastic pin. I preferred the silver color and made out my check accordingly.

The lesson here is that many people already want to contribute to your charity; they just need an opportunity. However, not any opportunity will do. People have preferred methods of making contributions. Some like to give through the mail; others will give only at their front door. Still others like to receive

How You Ask Makes the Difference

something of value for their contribution and will therefore attend dinners, auctions, and similar fund-raising events.

If you want to give everyone an opportunity to give to your charity, then you may have to be in several different places in order to be ready when they are interested in making the gift. That's my favorite aspect of fund raising. It's not as easy as it looks, and on occasion, you have to be clever!

Fund Raising 101

Part Two

Chapter Nine

Fund-Raising Methods

Three methods are used in fund raising. Most conventional fund raisers group the methods into these three broad categories, often referred to as the tripod: annual giving, capital campaigning, and planned giving.

Planned giving and capital campaigning are the only two fund-raising methods that stand alone. No one tries to make them into more than what they are.

On the other hand, annual giving is the most versatile method, having several distinct categories that include, but are not limited to direct mail, door-to-door soliciting, special events, cause marketing, grant writing, business and industry drives, plus marketing. In many large development offices, it's not uncommon to find a different staff person assigned to each of these categories. Following is a brief explanation of each category:

Direct mail is the practice of building a mail-responsive pool of people who contribute on being asked by request letter.

Door-to-door giving is solicitation such as the Mother's March conducted by the March of Dimes and Heart Sunday conducted by the Heart Association.

Fund Raising 101

The special event type of fund raising can take on any form that your imagination can dream up. Examples are any kind of an a-thon, black-tie events, jail-and-bail, garage sales, standing on your head, etc., etc., etc. Special events are normally considered to be events that the public pays to participate in. We conduct a rubber duck race, jail-and-bail, a kite event (people pay a dollar to put their name on a piece of paper and the paper is hung up on the premises of some sort of retail outlet), plus other special events.

I have heard of logging events, car washes, rummage sales, and dances. One of my comical favorites is cow-patty bingo. The only limits to special events are staying within the law and the creativity of the people involved.

Cause marketing takes place when a business of any type or size uses advertising dollars to underwrite a fund-raising project. As a result of the project, the involved charity receives some part of the purchase price. One of the best examples of a cause marketing project is when a company agrees to contribute a certain amount to the charity when a consumer purchases its product.

Grant writing usually consists of one activity--that of crafting a written proposal to be sent or taken to a business or foundation from which you are requesting financial support for a specific program.

Business and industry drives are a method of fund raising that is usually conducted by several business people, each of whom agrees to call on other businesses within their community. For best results, it is wise not to assign more than five businesses per caller. The thinking is that if the job is not too large, the caller is more likely to complete the assignment.

It Can Get Confusing

I realize that it can get confusing to talk about annual giving as one technique and turn right around and talk about it as being

Fund-Raising Methods

made up of several techniques. When I began this chapter, I hoped to clear up this confusion. Remember, the tripod of giving methods consists of only three. When talking about the various ways to raise funds, there are several. Eight is only my number; someone else might say there are more.

To further add to the confusion, you may find yourself at a fund-raising conference where you meet a person who has, as a job responsibility, some combination of methods that we haven't even discussed.

There are many variables, but you need to understand as much as you can. Sooner or later you will meet someone who has a fund-raising title that isn't clear to you. When that happens, maybe you won't be surprised.

When I arrived at the hospital where I currently work, I discovered that direct mail and business and industry campaigns were incorporated into two special events: a black-tie event and a telethon. It was somewhat unconventional, but it could work. All I needed to do was figure out how to manage it so that it would grow. That didn't take very long.

Let's get back to the other categories.

As I mentioned earlier, the types of fund raising discussed are all included in annual giving. The next two are stand-alone types of fund raising and are not as confusing, because of exceptions.

Planned giving is the act of making a financial contribution of an amount large enough to require a professional's advice in order to be the most effective.

Capital campaigns are slightly limited. They are generally thought to be events that occur only occasionally, not usually more often than once every five years. The funds raised during a capital campaign are used for a capital expenditure, such as a building or very expensive equipment. Sometimes, a capital campaign is conducted to raise endowment funds.

Fund Raising 101

I realize that <u>marketing</u> is not fund raising, but it is a commonly held opinion that fund-raising events are not going to be successful if they don't include marketing. Therefore, be sure to include a marketing component in every fund-raising event that you undertake. Marketing is a form of merchandizing or favorably displaying your organization for the purpose of gaining sales (support). This also applies to selling tickets to a special event.

That's my list of the eight types of fund raising. Just remember that if you ever sit for certification, there are only three: annual, planned, and capital.

In the following chapters, we expand on each of the fund-raising categories.

NOTE: Throughout this book, and in most conferences and learning opportunities, fund raising is usually referred to as a project. Anything else is usually referred to as a program.

Related Material

Within two years of entering the fund-raising profession, I had already discovered that there are three elements necessary in every fund raising project if it is to achieve its maximum effectiveness. These three elements are fund raising, friend making, and education.

I can't even imagine conducting a project that didn't have as its primary goal the raising of funds. Yet, it is as common as rain to hear a fund raiser say, "We weren't trying to make money this year; we were trying to make friends."

Making friends is a worthy secondary goal and I hope to make friends in every project, but education is also important, and it too is a secondary goal. If you are to become a bona fide fund-raising professional, you must overcome any hesitancy or embarrassment that you may have when it comes to asking people for financial support. That's the number one reason that we exist.

For a long time, government and the business community have known that charities get more from a dollar than either of them are able to. Yet, if we have no money, we have no ability to operate. I would have great difficulty in asking for money for myself. I am embarrassed to ask the bank for a loan to buy a car. However, I'm not embarrassed in the least when asking for support to buy a child a pair of glasses or to purchase a wheelchair for an elderly person.

Be Honest with Volunteers

Always be candid with your volunteers. If a project doesn't have good potential for raising funds, don't waste time, yours or theirs. Once you have that straight in your mind, you are ready to get serious. Ask yourself this question:

What financial, manpower, staff, and other resources will be necessary to conduct this project?

Once you have answered this question, you are ready to make the plunge. Fund raising is always my first goal, and I don't lose any sleep about assigning it the highest priority.

Failing Versus Creativity

If you are to be a successful fund raiser, you must learn to tolerate an occasional failure. There are so many variables involved in most fund-raising projects that no one person can be responsible for everything that goes wrong. If you are to become a good fund-raiser, you need to be willing to experiment, to be creative, to be daring.

When a volunteer wants to try something that you think is hair-brained, be willing to talk about it. Determine the cost, manpower, staff time, and whatever else is needed. If the risk is acceptable, go for it! If not, ask the chairman of the board for a committee to investigate the options.

A Nonfailing Failure

"If you're not making mistakes in your work, it's because you're not doing anything." This phrase was told to me in 1987 by the chairman of St. Francis Medical Center while I was directing their capital campaign.

Fund Raising 101

Failing isn't necessarily failing in fund raising if you learn from it. If you pay attention during the process, you will learn. But as far as I'm concerned, learning usually has a cost. It can be the cost of a book, or the cost of a meeting, or the cost of putting on a failure. I don't enjoy failing, I don't even want to fail, I just realize that with any thoughtful work that you do, some learning can take place.

A Statue in Front of NSFRE Headquarters

Four years ago, one of my co-workers, Pete Mishler, and I came up with what I believed to be an original idea. As far as I knew, it had never been done before. Ohhhh, what a day that was, my first brainchild. When I explained it to Pete, he was as sure as I was that we were going to be in the fund-raising hall of fame! We would be as immortal as Sy Seymour. There would be books written about us. Fund raisers would talk about us in seminars and workshops. We stopped just short of imagining a statue being erected in front of the National Society of Fund Raising Executives (NSFRE) Headquarters. What was this brainchild?

A kite-a-thon! That's right a kite-a-thon. It's laughable today. We had envisioned distributing kites to the eight Wal-Mart stores and one Sam's store that work with us in Northeast Tennessee and Southwest Virginia. We imagined two, three, even four hundred youngsters with their parents flying kites all on the same day in April. We reasoned that these children would acquire sponsors for $10, $20, even $30 for every hour that they could keep their kites aloft. Now, on the surface, this seems like a pretty reasonable idea, doesn't it?

Before we go on with the kite-a-thon, I need to explain to you about the Wal-Mart angels. They are better known as Miracle Workers. Each Wal-Mart store has one of them and their responsibility is to represent the store manager in their work with local charities and the community. Although most are women, there are some men Miracle Workers. I don't know how they are selected, but I can assure you they can work miracles. The Miracle Worker nearest our office is a wonderful women by the name of Fay Ferguson. She was already a Miracle Worker when I came to Northeast Tennessee, over five years ago, and she is still there as I finish this book.

Pete and I called Fay and invited her to our office to hear about our brainchild. Because we knew this idea was to become our signature project, we sold it to her with a fury. In all fairness, she loved the idea as much as we did. After she agreed, we invested several hundred dollars on the purchase of specially designed kites, with Wal-Mart's name, other sponsors names, and our hospital's name all over them. Then we set about distributing them with pledge forms and other materials.

After all this planning and work, *we had fewer than a dozen children participate.* My signature project was a complete failure.

In case you have forgotten, a few paragraphs earlier, we were talking about being experimental, creative, even daring. We were all those things and still experienced a flat-out failure. But that wasn't my first failure, nor is it likely to be my last! On the other hand, we experienced many successes here, especially with the help and involvement of Wal-Mart's Miracle Workers. We conducted wrestling matches, bake sales, raffles, special nights at the dirt-track car races, roller-skating, and many more.

Lifetime Giving Cycle

It's important that fund raisers understand that people give to charities in different ways throughout their lives. There are many reasons for these variations, but the primary reasons are the source and quantity of their income. The cycle begins at the approximate age of twenty-five. The couple is young and they have a young family. Usually, the only resources they have at their disposal are those that come to them from employment. Therefore, if they are interested in supporting charities, their gifts are likely to be small and given from their usually small disposable income. The average income for these younger couples is from the high teens to the midthirties (in thousands). (See Figure 11.)

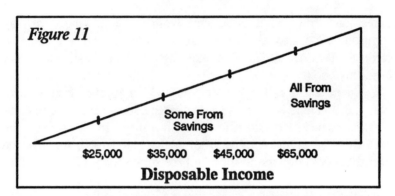

Disposable Income

Gifts given by younger people generally come from employment income. Later in life, gifts tend to come from accumulated assets. An appreciated asset is any property of value that was bought for one price and its value has increased since its purchase.

By the time the average couple reaches the age of thirty-five, their income has risen to a range that begins in the midtwenties and usually tops out in the midforties. Although their gifts to charity can still come from work income, many times they are also able to give from accumulated assets. Their accumulated assets might consist of rental property, or an inheritance, or they may elect to contribute using an insurance product. It's not unusual for individuals in this age bracket to begin to support capital campaigns.

When the average couple reaches the age of fifty-five or greater, they begin to think of retirement and they will not be as likely to make contributions from their working income. At this stage in life, they often have appreciated assets and are ready, willing, and more likely to make gifts from these assets.

This same couple, if they have retired, may no longer be willing to make a cash gift because they may be concerned about their income stream. At this stage, their income stream consists of interest from investments, rental property, Social Security, and retirement accounts. And remember, if they are retired, they are usually living on a lower income than they had when working.

Fund-Raising Methods

Planning

Planning your fund-raising projects and programs is essential to success. With good planning, you can manage dozens of activities annually. Without planning, you will be lucky to have any success at all.

One of the greatest lessons I learned about planning came from my Jaycee days. We were preparing to conduct a "Let-George-Do-It, Day." You know how you are always hearing people say, "I know it needs doing, but let George do it." This is just another way of passing the buck. Our Jaycee chapter had borrowed several National Guard tents to be erected on the parking lot of a large new mall in my hometown of North Little Rock, Arkansas.

We intended to pitch the tents and in each would be several activities that are not always convenient to get to, such as voter registration, registration and vaccinations for pets, flu shots, have your home checked for radon gas, eye tests, and so on.

George Day was to start at 10:00 A.M. Several of us arrived at about 6:30 A.M. to begin erecting the tents. By 8:30, all twelve of us had huffed, puffed, cussed, kicked the ground, and many other terrible things, but we still didn't have the first tent erected. (This is one of. my Sam Robbins stories.) Sam was the president of our Jaycee chapter and a bridge engineer by training. Although we had been there since 6:30, he didn't arrive until 8:35. He parked his car and began slowing unfolding his long frame from the small car onto the parking lot. Sam never got in a hurry.

I rushed over to Sam and said, "Where the ---- ---- have you been? We've been out here for hours and these tents won't go up. No matter what we do to them, they won't go up." Sam meandered over to where one of the tents still lay in a neatly rolled-up ball. And why not, we hadn't even touched that one yet.

Sam sat down, seemingly oblivious to my anger or the jeers coming from the other monkeys we had become. In less than three minutes, Sam stood up and began unrolling the tent. He seemed to know exactly what he was doing. I said to myself, "He can't know what he's doing, he just can't."

Fund Raising 101

In another two or three minutes he had the entire tent spread out on the ground and had stakes laid at each corner. He waved over one of the Jaycees who was as awestruck as I was. In a flash, up came one corner of the tent. Sam went to the other end and called over another Jaycee, and in seconds up went another corner. You've figured this out already, haven't you?

In an effort not to be left out, I ran over and grabbed a pole on the last corner of the tent. When Sam came close to me, he whispered in my ear, "Read the instructions first, you dumb butt!" I grinned; he was right. Within an hour, we had all ten tents up and ready for George Day. Such a little thing, yet without reading the instructions, many things cannot be done.

Planning a fund-raising event is like that. If properly done, planning provides an economy of time and manpower. Everything that you need will be there where you need it and when you want it. It will even be in the right quantity.

Now, what does planning or having a failed project or putting up tents have to do with types of gifts? Maybe not much, but fund raising isn't just about books and tools, or gifts of cash or thank-you notes. It's about many things, like love of humankind. It's about children and old folks. It's about learning and growing. As another of my mentors said, "It's about serial reciprocity. The act of taking what you have learned and sharing it with others who can benefit by your experiences. Serial reciprocity--if you have been given something of value, you must pass it along."

I give to you the wisdom of Sam Robbins, "Read the instructions first, you dumb butt!"

Chapter Ten

Annual Giving

Read definitions at the end of chapter
before beginning Chapter Ten.

****

This chapter is exciting because it deals with the one aspect of fund raising that we all face: locating operational funds. We discuss what annual giving is, how it fits into the development process, why it is important to your charity, and we lay out the organization of an uncomplicated annual campaign.

Annual giving, sometimes referred to as current giving, is the backbone of the development process. It serves in building the relationships that are necessary for your charity to succeed. Also, it provides the operating revenue for the ongoing activities and programs of your institution. In other words, it pays the lights, water, gas, and rent, as well as the salaries of the staff. All other forms of fund raising--capital campaigning, planned giving, special events, and so on--very often feed from the volunteers recruited and trained on the annual campaign projects. If your charity does not have a solid annual giving program, you need to get started right away.

There is no one definition of the annual campaign that you could use that would get a half-dozen senior fund raisers to agree on.

Fund Raising 101

I like the following: Annual giving is intended to solicit financial support on an annual or repeating basis from the same, yet widening, donor base. The funds may be used at the discretion of the board but are generally considered to be operating funds.

Annual giving is normally the method by which first-time donors enter your donor pool. Many professional fund raisers use the annual campaign to teach repeat giving. They do this by using such fund-raising techniques as direct mail and phon-a-thons. Direct face-to-face asking for the gift is by far the most successful method for securing gifts. Using whatever volunteers you have available, call first on as many of your prospects as you can manage with those volunteers. Follow up with a phon-a-thon to those you could not call on in person, and use direct mail for the rest. An outline of a face-to-face campaign comes later in this chapter.

Once an individual or business becomes a donor, you then have the responsibility to familiarize them with your charity, involve them in its activities, and move them up to higher levels of giving in what we referred to earlier as the Pyramid of Giving. (See Figure 12.)

I use the Pyramid of Giving in training my volunteers for two reasons. First, it illustrates the continuous need for new donors to be brought into the donor pool. It is estimated that approximately 20 percent of your current donors will not give your charity a gift next year. If your charity is to grow at all, you need at least a 21 percent increase in the number of new donors added to your donor pool each year. Second, the Pyramid demonstrates that it takes 80 percent of all your donors to generate 20 percent of your charity's revenue. On the other hand, 20 percent of your donors will equal 80 percent of your charity's revenue.

I agree with the first reason, but I have never experienced an exact 80 percent to 20 percent split. However, I do agree with the theory. In the years that I had annual giving as part of my overall responsibility, it was always in the ballpark of the 80 to 20 percent split.

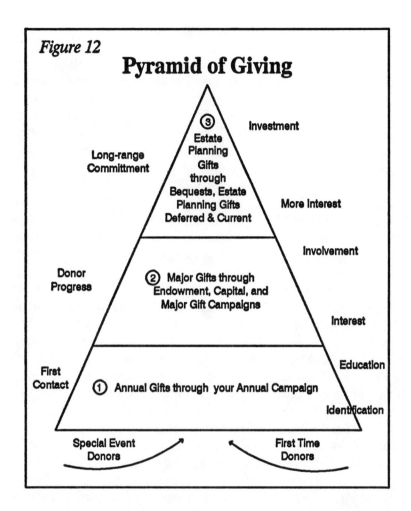

Figure 12

Pyramid of Giving

The Pyramid of Giving (Figure 12) is divided into four dollar groupings, $5 to $99, $100 to $999, $1,000 to $9,999, and $10,000 and up. The lowest grouping usually represents first time entry-level gifts, and the larger amounts represent the growth that takes place as the donor becomes more knowledgeable and involved with your charity. You may use any figures you wish in a pyramid that represents your charity, $1 to $49, $50 to $250, and so on.

Fund Raising 101

There are many ways by which a suspect or prospect can be brought into the charity's donor pool during the annual campaign. These methods include, but are not limited to, phon-a-thons, personal appeals (i.e., business drives and door-to-door solicitations), special events, cause marketing, tel-a-thons, merchandise sales, and direct mail. Direct mail seems to be the one being used by the largest number of charities.

Let's assume that we have 100 new donors who wish to support our organization by responding to a mail solicitation. These 100 gifts vary from $5 to $99. It is generally felt that a gift of less than $5 in today's economy actually costs your charity money to handle. For our illustration, 100 donors give at least $5 but not more than $99.

Any charity receiving a gift in any amount should assume that the donor has some interest in the charity or at least the program that is being funded by a project. Now that we have these new donors with confirmed names and addresses, we want to thank them as soon as possible. It would be nice if we could do so in the next day's mail. If you can do that, then do it. It's not always possible for us to do that at our foundation. But we do get the thank-you notes out as quickly as we can, rarely longer than two working days.

The thank-you notes are the first contact with your new donor. You want the thank-you letter to be well written and to assure donors that they have joined a charity that is (1) supported by many others, (2) is grateful to its supporters and (3) is fiscally responsible. The letter might look something like this: (See Figure 13.)

Your letter can be longer or shorter than the example and may include many more niceties. The example points out the three things that should positively go into a thank-you letter.

Signing this type of letter is very important because it starts with "I." I would never start a letter in this manner if I were going to sign it. My intention is to have one of the children who benefits from the ABC Project sign the letter.

Figure 13

Dear Mr. and Mrs. Donor:

I would like to express my personal gratitude to you for your support of the ABC Project. Your gift, along with that of others who also see the need, will ensure that we reach the goal.

Please be assured that your investment in the ABC Project will be carefully spent to ensure that these children have exactly what we said they would have.

In 1988, I attended an NSFRE Regional meeting in Atlanta. It was the first time in my career that I was going to be near enough to where the Certified Fund Raising Executive (CFRE) exam was being offered, to sit for it. One day, I arrived late for lunch, and the roundtable discussions had already begun. Looking around, I saw only one empty seat. I was reluctant to take the seat because there were only young women sitting at the table, and I had hoped to sit near one of my idols who was also attending the meeting.

Hesitantly, I took the chair and smiled and nodded to those who had noticed my late arrival at the table. Hardly had I gotten the napkin to my lap when I was awarded the finest idea that I received during the entire conference.

These young women were all Campfire Girl staff. This was also my first exposure to this wonderful organization. One of the women, three chairs around the table from me on my left, said to the woman on my immediate right, "My daughter brought home a note from her leader last week that said, 'thanks for the $10 gift'." "That was it," she said. The woman on my right said, "I have the girls sign all the letters we send out, sometimes I even have them write them first and then sign them."

You probably already know that it is many times more effective to have the people who benefit from the program sign the thank-you letters. Well, I must have been holed up in a cave or something. That had not occurred to me.

Fund Raising 101

Since having the privilege of overhearing that conversation, I rarely sign a thank-you letter. Think what an effect it would have on the donors to various boys clubs to have the boys sign the thank-you letters. Or, how about a letter signed by a recovered addict who has managed to stay clean for twelve months. Get the idea?

Let's get back to the thank-you letter as your first contact with your new donor. Depending on your manpower and the methods you have available to you, your next contact with your new donor is crucial. Some of the methods of following up include an invitation to attend an open house or a personal tour of your facility, a newsletter, newspaper clippings about the ABC Project, and the like. You have now begun the education of and involvement of your $5 donor in your charity's activities. Once this has been done, and assuming the donor is having a good experience, you are now ready to invite the donor to participate in a project or program.

We are acting on the premise that everything is ideal and works perfectly. It rarely does. Yet, all you are doing is being polite and you can't get into much trouble being polite. I have activated many volunteers by doing no more than talking to them at an open house and asking them if they would be willing to help if I could find something interesting for them to do. I have always believed in the cause that my charity stands for, which enables me to be honest and straightforward with people about what I needed and how they could help.

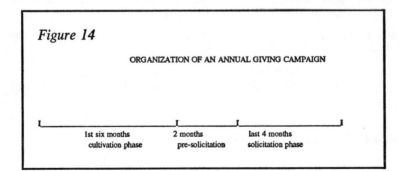

Figure 14

ORGANIZATION OF AN ANNUAL GIVING CAMPAIGN

1st six months	2 months	last 4 months
cultivation phase	pre-solicitation	solicitation phase

At this point, we should look at how the annual giving revenue is organized into the annual campaign. Our example is a simple version. You can add to it as your experience and sophistication grow. (See Figure 14.)

Our goal is to raise $50,000 for the ABC Program. We are going to assume that we can locate 100 suspects (a suspect is a person or business who is likely to provide financial support if asked by the right person). We will evaluate the suspects and in this case, determine that 75 will remain as evaluated prospects (a suspect is promoted to prospect after the evaluation team determines that the suspect has good enough cause to supply financial support). Don't get hung up over the differences between suspects and prospects. There isn't enough difference to get bent out of shape over, but there are many practicing fund raisers who make the distinction.

The Cultivation Phase

The cultivation phase takes place during the first six months of your campaign year. If your year is July to June, it still happens in the first six months. Several things must be done during this time.

First Six Months
1. Identify suspects
2. Evaluation of suspects
3. Seventy-five prospects remain
4. Research the prospects (this is sometimes done while the person is still a suspect)
5. Recruitment of workers
6. Provide training for the workers
7. Determine what written materials will be needed
8. Begin the cultivation meeting for the prospects

The suspects who were assigned values through the evaluation process are now prospects. Research is done on each prospect, gathering as much information as possible. The evaluation and research steps are very sensitive subjects. Allow only very trustworthy persons to be involved in these two processes. I would advise that the only staff member to participate in the evaluation and rating session be the executive director, who should immediately take charge of the research information and put it under lock and key.

If we wish to reach our goal of $50,000, we will want a giving chart, which will look something like the one below. The giving chart will be handed to the prospect at the time of the solicitation. The caller can hand the chart over to the prospect and say something like, "Mr. Jones, if the ABC Program is to become a success, we need to locate people who are able to contribute a sum of money equal to one of those indicated on the giving chart. Do you think you could give one of the larger amounts?" (See Figure 15.)

Figure 15

The ABC Program Giving Chart
$50,000 Goal

# of Gift(s)	Gift Size	Running Total
1	10,000	$10,000
2	5,000	20,000
3	2,500	27,500
4	1,000	31,500
10 gifts totaling about half of the goal		31,500
Second half will look something like		
6	750	36,000
10	500	41,000
10	400	45,000
10	300	48,000
Many gifts of $100 and other sizes	2,000	$50,000

Fifty or so of the seventy-five prospects must become donors for you to reach the goal of $50,000. One gift of $10,000 is important along with other sizable gifts, ending with fifty total gifts. Fifty out of seventy-five is on the high end of successful calls on prospects. In fact, it will require 1.5 to 2 well-cultivated prospects to receive one gift. With only seventy-five prospects, the odds are that you will not reach your $50,000 goal. You have two choices: to go on and do the best you can or to gather additional suspects to become prospects. In this case study, we are going forward with what we have.

A poorly cultivated prospect pool will require three to five prospects per one gift. How do we go about cultivating our prospect pool? Through cultivation meetings. At a workshop in July 1992, a consultant from New Jersey referred to cultivation meetings as parlor meetings. I had forgotten that we used to call them that. I fell in love again with the term, so I will use it from this point on.

What is a parlor meeting?

A parlor meeting happens when a couple invites approximately five couples into their home. A 15- to 30-minute talk about the charity's case for support is presented sometime during the evening. The rest of the time the host couple entertains with food, music, and so on. The host couple determines the entertainment. Sometimes the presentation can consist of thought-provoking questions such as: what would we do if this organization didn't exist in our community? Or, is our community the better for having the ABC Charity conduct its activities here?

Often, the hosts come from the prospect pool; more often they are board members who agree to be the hosts. It's very helpful if the hosts become the workers in a few months when it's time to make the solicitation calls. And it is helpful if the hosts and workers are influential people in the community. Last, they must be willing to make a solid gift. I use the word solid rather than substantial because the hosts should contribute as meaningful a gift as possible.

It is not absolutely necessary that the hosts become workers but you can see the advantages. I have always made sure the hosts understood the advantage they would have by doing both. No matter what you say or do, not all will take on both roles.

The hosts can look at the remaining names in the pool and select around five people or couples to invite to their home for a parlor meeting. There is no solicitation at a parlor meeting, only education in the form of the aforementioned talk about the charity's case for support. A video or film can be substituted for some of the time. It is hoped that the prospects leave at the end of the evening having had a nice time and feeling good about learning more about your organization.

Caution! Resist any attempt on the part of the guests (prospects) to contribute while they are attending the parlor meetings. Tell them that you are gratified that they wish to support the ABC Program but that you would appreciate their allowing someone to call on them at a more appropriate time. They will usually concede.

If appropriate, make arrangements for the guests to visit the ABC Program in person sometime before the end of the cultivation phase. If you are able to arrange this visit, the prospect will be even better informed and more likely to make a substantial gift when the solicitation call is made. If a visit doesn't take place, try to communicate in other ways what is going on or planned.

The Pre-Solicitation Stage

Next comes the pre-solicitation phase. During this time, the workers select the prospects on whom they wish to call. It is very likely that they will call on the prospects who attended their parlor meeting but not necessarily. A worker should always attempt to call on those prospects whom they feel confident they can influence.

There are all kinds of influences--wealth and power are the ones that come to mind most often. However, don't overlook owed favors, "I gave to your charity last time".

If training is available, it should take place during the pre-solicitation phase. "How You Ask Makes The Difference" is a good tool and is found in Chapter 8. The workers should familiarize themselves with the case statement and any background materials or information about the prospect that you have concerning past giving, connection with your charity, and so on.

In a hospital campaign a few years ago, I participated in the training of a worker who was to call on the wealthiest businessman in the entire community. The worker had been grinding through his presentation for over thirty minutes when it finally occurred to him that the businessman wasn't listening. He stopped abruptly and said, *"Mr. Jones, you aren't paying the slightest attention to me, why?"* Mr. Jones' answer was straight to the point, *"Why hell, Bob, my daughter has been head nurse on A-7 for six years. If you ever get around to telling me what you want, I'll give it to ya!"* We did our homework and still missed this important piece of information. Try not to let this happen to you. It sure makes you look bad.

And finally, the workers receive the pledge cards of the prospects on whom they are to call, with the assigned evaluation and any other personal information.

The Solicitation Phase

The solicitation phase occurs when the workers make their calls on their prospects. It's helpful if a written case statement can be handed to the prospect along with a giving chart. The worker should be patient and answer any and all questions that the prospect asks. Again, refer to "How You Ask" for the remainder of the call.

The appropriate thank-you letter should follow the visit to thank the prospect for the time or the gift, whichever is relevant.

Other Types of Fund Raising During the Annual Campaign

Other types of fund raising fit agreeably into the time-line for annual giving. Special events can be worked into the cultivation phase, and direct mail and phon-a-thons fit nicely at the end of the solicitation phase.

Remember, you can improve your chances of receiving a gift if you do the proper research, evaluate correctly, involve influential people to make the calls, have a compelling written case statement, and have a clear giving chart.

You can find suspects anywhere, but I would start with current givers, clients, and non-givers among my constituency, volunteers, former clients, and vendors. Other likely prospects can come from potential clients, friends of clients or givers, businesses, and individuals.

Don't forget that there are many other forms of fund raising that can be incorporated into your annual fund drive, including phon-a-thons, personal appeals (i.e., business drives, and door-to-door solicitations), special events, cause marketing, tel-a-thons, merchandise sales, and direct mail.

****

Definitions:
- ☞ A prospect is someone who is considered to have the capability but may or may not give you your next gift.
- ☞ A suspect is someone who has not yet been determined able to give you your next gift and who may or may not do so.
- ☞ A donor or giver is any person, business, corporation, foundation, and the like that has given you a gift.
- ☞ Project usually refers to fund raising, and program usually refers to an activity that is not fund raising. An example of a program might be delivering for Meals On Wheels.
- ☞ A worker is a person who makes solicitation calls on prospects.
- ☞ A parlor meeting occurs when workers invite couples to their home for refreshments and an educational experience about your charity.
- ☞ A case statement is a compelling story about the program for which money is to be raised.
- ☞ To evaluate or rate a suspect is to have a group of not more than five people, who generally know almost everyone in town, discuss the suspects and assign a value to each of

Annual Giving

them. The value represents their collective assessment of what the suspect could give if appealed to on behalf of a project. The evaluation and rating group is promised anonymity and is usually made up of people who are extremely knowledgeable about the community. After the suspects have been evaluated, they become prospects. Those not assigned a value remain suspect or are dropped from the suspect list.

Fund Raising 101

Chapter Eleven

Phon-a-thons and Memorials

The definition of telemarketing is raising funds by selling products or services by telephone. Many charities conduct a phon-a-thon as part of their annual campaign. Colleges in particular are masters of phon-a-thon techniques because they have the three main ingredients readily accessible to make it work:

1. Many phones with separate lines (ten is a good number).
2. A constituency (their alumni).
3. People willing to make the calls (such as students and/or teachers).

Almost any charity can organize a phon-a-thon. We have an annual phon-a-thon at our hospital. We gain access to places with ten or more phones by asking local banks, insurance companies, or any other organization that has ten phones that we may use.

We consider the entire community to be our constituency. However, we call only previous donors of under $100. Our list contains all donors who has given to us over the past four years. Once a donor reaches a gift level of $100, we move them to a list that requires them to be called on in person.

Fund Raising 101

We ask local businesses that have employees who are accustomed to doing business over the phone to put together a team of ten people to make the solicitation calls. Banks, insurance companies, stockbrokers, and real estate firms do a lot of business over the phone. Because of this, their personnel make excellent phone solicitors. After we have recruited ten teams with a captain and ten members on each team, we bring the captains together for orientation and training.

Furnishing a measure of competition between the teams adds fun and creates a little esprit de corps. The owners of the various real estate and insurance companies usually enjoy the competition and cheer their teams on. A rotating trophy is provided, with the winning team keeping it from one year to the next. A top prize is awarded to the team that raises the most money. There is also a prize for the top individual money raiser and the individual who has the largest number of pledges.

Elsewhere in this book, we have discussed the various methods of making visits with prospective donors or previous donors. We remind you that a face-to-face visit is by far the best method of asking for financial support. However, the telephone is considered second by many fund raisers, especially if the callers call the same persons they called the year before.

Although telephone solicitation is second, there is a caveat. The caveat is that the donors or prospective donors must have a connection with the charity that is being represented. Example: "Mr. Donor, you contributed last year, can we count on your support again this year?" The connection is that the prospect gave last year. Another connection might be that the prospects know the callers from some association with them. If cold calls are made by a charity that the prospects have not previously supported, it is debatable as to whether a phone contact is the second-best method.

Phon-a-thons, often referred to as telemarketing, have become so prevalent in our country that many people answer their phones only after their answer machine has kicked in and they can hear the caller's voice. My daughter was a telemarketer and I want to be

114

sympathetic, but any sign of cooperation to a telemarketer is seen as an opportunity to make a sale. All I want to do is keep from being rude. It's not easy.

If the phone solicitor is representing a recognized charity, especially one that the prospect has supported in the past, usually the caller can get the message out and gain the desired support.

In this case, the prospect connects with the caller and may even ask questions about the charity. It's not unusual for the caller and the prospect already to be acquainted. In these cases, the telephone call takes on an air of a personal visit. This type of contact is healthy for the charity. The caller becomes an extension of your charity and adds a measure of prestige to your charity.

The callers often bring new donors to your organization by pre-calling family members and friends, schools and places of worship, acquaintances, coworkers, civic club members, and anyone else they can think of. These new donors are a bonus because they come to your organization without a prospecting cost.

Phon-a-thons have been consistently good at gaining revenue. We take out the donors of $100 or greater for face-to-face visits, yet our phon-a-thon results have grown from $12,000 to over $35,000 in five years.

One of the reasons that our phon-a-thon yield has grown is that we have been able to persuade donors to increase the size of their gifts. Donors of $5 and $10 are increased to $25 by simply asking. Donors of $25 are increased to $35, then $40, then $50, with little more than a request. The phon-a-thon is a wonderful tool for upgrading the gifts of most donors.

Another plus for phon-a-thons includes the ability to learn what it is about your charity that causes donors to support it. All you need to do is have the solicitors ask, "*May I ask what it is about the Adult Handicapped Center that you support?*" You may find that the donors have a handicapped child or are handicapped themselves. There are any number of reasons. By including this question, you may locate future volunteers.

Fund Raising 101

Phon-A-Thon Prospects

Where do the phon-a-thon prospects fit on the giving pyramid? Of course, it depends partially on their giving level, but you have begun to educate these donors and they know enough to qualify as second-level donors. More often than not they can be classified as middle-class by income and other criteria.

If you are forced to make cold calls, you will have some success but much less. The public is growing weary of telemarketing, and you only add to that problem when you engage in cold calling.

Successes of Phon-A-Thons

Some of the reasons you will have success are based on the fact that a certain number of people are telephone responsive. With these people in particular, the phon-a-thon can be used as an effective marketing tool. Not only can you solicit by phone, but you can talk about some of the products or services your institution has to offer the public. As an additional bonus, you save mail costs.

A phon-a-thon can be an effective method for your institution to test market a new product or service that it wants to offer to the public.

Two Approaches

Most phon-a-thons follow one of two procedures when preparing for their kickoff. Either they are going to make cold calls or they are going to send a letter in advance telling the prospect that they will be calling during a certain period. We have already discussed the disadvantages of making cold calls.

By alerting the prospect by letter that a volunteer will be calling during a certain time, prospects tend not to be as irritated by the inconvenience of the call. Once the call has been completed, a statement should be mailed to the donor verifying the pledge that was made over the phone. A statement can be made up in advance so that the callers can write quick thank-you note and sign their name, thus personalizing the statement.

Phon-A-Thons and Memorials

Paid Volunteers

The term *paid volunteers* is a redundancy. Volunteers are no longer volunteers if they accept pay. But this is a dilemma. Many charities would like to begin a phon-a-thon and conduct it annually. However, some smaller charities do not have a large enough cadre of volunteers. So, if your charity doesn't and you want to begin a phon-a-thon, is it okay to hire phone solicitors?

This is a difficult question. If there were no other way and my charity needed the cash, I would probably hire people. Colleges often hire their students as a means to provide student assistance. It's not wrong, but there are so many telemarketing schemes going on around the country, I would avoid it if possible.

Volunteers help to keep the cost down, but paid staff are much easier to control. You can tell staff when to come in, how long to stay, where to call, and what to say. But you lose the esprit de corps, the prestige of having particular volunteers, the contacts they bring with them, and a lot more.

Preparing the Callers

The callers cannot operate in a vacuum; they need to be trained and trained properly. The more informed they are about your institution, the better job they can do. We start by bringing in the captains, touring them through the hospital so that they know what it is they are raising money for. We talk about the incentives and the competition, and answer any questions they have.

Next, we go through the same procedure for the actual members of the teams, giving them the history of the institution and the history of the phon-a-thon.

On the night the callers begin, we give them a stack of cards with the prospects' name, address, and all past giving history. No matter what the prospect supports, even if it's not the phon-a-thon, the caller knows that. A suggested increase is included on the card, so that the solicitor will be able to go right to it at the appointed time.

117

Fund Raising 101

We provide a script for the phone solicitors to use and go over it with them, suggesting how it should be used. We also let them know that if they are more comfortable with changes, they may incorporate them. In preparing a script, simplicity is important.

The prospect should not be easily able to tell that the caller is using a script. People do not say "do not" when they are speaking, they say "don't." Be sure that you remember that kind of thing when preparing the script.

The rest of this chapter is made up of examples.

Following is a letter to the phon-a-thon volunteers. Be sure to thank them for agreeing to be on a team. Mail this letter to them after they have agreed to make calls but before the actual phon-a-thon. (See Figure 16.)

The following explanation is provided to every phone solicitor so that they are properly informed.

What Is a Phon-A-Thon?

A phon-a-thon is an efficient way to reach approximately 3,000 people who have previously given to the Adult Handicapped Center, using the help of teams of volunteer telephone callers like yourself. Our aim is to have each donor make a pledge again this year.

All prospective donors will receive a personalized letter encouraging them to say "yes" when you call to ask for their pledge.

A suggested letter to be mailed to prospects in advance of the phon-a-thon follows: (See Figure 17.)

Following are eight kinds of information that you can provide each caller on the night that their team is making calls:

1. Last Year's Phon-A-Thon

Last year's phon-a-thon raised $29,624 from 1,965 pledges. Eighty-nine volunteers from nine businesses and other organizations made calls to previous donors from sixteen counties in four states. The Second National Bank was the winner of the top-dollar trophy

118

Phon-A-Thons and Memorials

Figure 16

The Adult Handicapped Center
1994 Phon-a-thon
Chairman - Tom Porter

Dear Phon-a-thon Volunteer:

Thank you for being a part of this team. Without your help and enthusiasm, there would be no phon-a-thon. You make the difference. There is particular excitement about this year's fund-raising potential and how the dollars will be used--in helping with the expansion of services and the acquisition of a T-bol-lee.

We are very pleased that this year's Phon-a-thon has two new teams. We are also deeply appreciative of the donation by the First National Bank of the use of their offices and phone system for the event.

The attached information was designed to arm you with the facts and procedural guidelines so that you will be as effective as possible in getting pledges. Any comments or questions you might have regarding this material would be welcomed.

I wish you success and fun on the night your team makes calls. Thanks again for helping the handicapped adults in our community.

Warm regards,

Campaign Chairman's Name

---

with a whopping $6,320 raised. Second National was also the company with the greatest number of pledges: 309. Libby MacNamara of American Bank was the individual with the greatest number of pledges, 65, and the top individual dollars raised, $1,330.

2. Why A Phon-A-Thon?

The phon-a-thon is an important part of the Adult Handicapped Center's fund-raising effort. The average pledge is

---

Figure 17

Date

Name
Address

Dear (Name),

You can make a big difference in the life of a handicapped adult!

During the next few weeks, teams of volunteers will be calling and asking thousands of area residents who contributed last year to donate again. The response you give when we call could change the life of a handicapped person.

We are very grateful for your generosity in the past. As a result of your support and that of thousands of others in this region, many handicapped adults have been given a helping hand.

Many lives have been improved through the work of the Adult Handicapped Center. Important and badly needed equipment has been added to the Center. Because of your earlier support, these adults have been able to receive the help they needed right here in our community. They no longer have to travel to faraway cities and be away from their family and friends.

There is still more work to be done. With continued support by you and others, the Adult Handicapped Center is able to provide truly first-class quality care for all the handicapped adults of the Mountain Empire Region.

In a few days, when a volunteer calls, please consider making a pledge again. Your generosity will inspire others to give. All pledges will be used to kick off the campaign for the Adult Handicapped Home this year.

Sincerely,

Anne Chairperson
1994 Phon-a-thon Chairman

Phon-A-Thons and Memorials

$19.55 and represents 26 percent of our fund-raising income. The phon-a-thon has become a very important way to make personal contact with our donors to ask them to give again. Short of a personal visit, a phone call from a sincere and enthusiastic volunteer is the best possible way to raise funds.

3. Phon-A-Thon Facts

The average phon-a-thon caller made 50 attempted calls, averaging 34 completed calls. Of those completed calls, about 60 percent, or 30, resulted in pledges. With pledge amounts averaging about $20, the total dollars raised in an evening averaged just over $4,000.

This year's overall phon-a-thon goal is $36,000. With eight scheduled nights of calling, that's an average per night of over $4,500. If each team has ten callers, the average must be $450 per caller to reach our goal. At an average of $20 per pledge, that's 22.5 pledges. If the team has only eight callers, each caller will need to have 25 pledges of $22.50.

In setting your personal goals for the evening, remember that you can expect to dial the phone about three times for each pledge you receive (depending, of course, on your skill and luck).

PARTICIPATING TEAMS:
First National Bank
Carlton & Jones, CPAs
Fisher Real Estate
Second National Bank
Last Tennessee Bank
Two-Rivers Savings and Loan
Franklin Insurance Company
Hill Top Bank

Telephoning homes works best after the dinner hour and before it gets late into the evening. You will be fairly safe calling between 6:30 P.M. and 9:00 P.M. Any later than that, and you will get some pretty grumpy people.

Fund Raising 101

4. Schedule for the Evening of a Phon-A-Thon

6:00 P.M.	Team members arrive at First National Bank. Refreshments are served.
6:20 P.M.	Charity staff and team captain go over procedures with team members and answer questions.
6:45 P.M.	Calling begins.
8:30 P.M.	Free calling, if desired. Free calling is calling people not on your list (i.e., parents and friends)
9:01 P.M.	Thank you for helping!

5. The Winning Edge

The optional free calling time from 8:30 to 9:00 P.M. is a chance for you to call, and often obtain pledges from, anyone you wish. You may want to bring a prepared list of names and phone numbers with you. You may even want to bring out the pledges that you sandbagged earlier in the week!

Please do not call anyone from the "no call" list of names provided to you.

Give special thanks to the First National Bank for the use of their facilities.

6. Before You Call

Please read over each prospect card before dialing to become familiar with the person's name and past giving record. Also, please note the increased amount that you will ask for.

Gave previously:

    $10 to $15, ask for $20
    $20, ask for $25
    $25 or more, add 20 percent to previous gift amount

Also, review the sample pledge cards in this handout to become familiar with the procedure for completing the card.

Please feel free to use your own words when relating the Adult Handicapped Center's needs. There is no need to feel timid or shy. You are here tonight donating your time for this cause. This is impressive to us and will be to those you are calling.

7. Suggested Speech

"Hello, may I speak with (name on pledge card)? This is (caller's name). I'm with a group of volunteers calling on behalf of the Adult Handicapped Center in Franklin. (Name of person), the Adult Handicapped Center greatly appreciated your support last year. This year's funds will be used to purchase a T-bol-lee, a machine that builds upper body strength. *"We'd like to ask you to help out again this year with a gift of ($$).*" *"Can you help us with ($$)?"*

Phoning Suggestions
    Prospect says "YES"

"That's wonderful! Let me express the sincere thanks of everyone at the Adult Handicapped Center for your support. We'll mail you a pledge card and return envelope. Is your correct address (check address on card)? Thank you again, (person's name), for your gift. It will be used right here in our community"

Prospect Is Undecided (gives soft yes)
"I will send you a pledge form and return envelope for you to use if you decide to make a pledge. Thank you for your consideration."

Unspecified Response
"May I put you down, (person's name), for the same amount as last year? That would be ($$)."

"I just sent a gift"
Find out if the gift was for a memorial, a regular pledge payment, or was made for some other reason. Please record information on the pledge card.

Fund Raising 101

<u>Prospect says "NO"</u>
"We will miss your support, but we understand your situation completely. Thank you again for your past support of (Charity)."

8) General Tips

☞   Be sure to verify address.

☞   If someone complains about the (charity), the (charity's) staff member should handle the call.

☞   Most important, **<u>HAVE FUN!!!</u>**

Memorial Giving

Many charities offer memorial giving as a means for the public to provide support of their work. There may be charities that do not lend themselves readily to this method of fund raising. However, for those of you interested in memorial giving, I will outline the process. You can then determine whether or not you wish to use it.

Memorial giving often starts with the local funeral homes. While the funeral arrangements are being made, the funeral director asks the family representative if the family would like to recognize a particular charity in the death announcement. The death announcement that you see in the newspaper is usually taken care of by the funeral home.

Many charities provide the funeral homes and doctors' offices with a tastefully prepared pamphlet asking for the family's support in a diplomatic way. It is particularly easy to suggest supporting the cancer fund if the deceased died of cancer. I doubt that many charities have received support as a result of simply having pamphlets in funeral homes. But having the pamphlets there serves as a reminder to the funeral directors and family members.

The method most commonly used by charities for memorials is a specially designed envelope with wording similar to the following: (See Figure 18 for wording for a memorial phamplet.)

Phon-A-Thons and Memorials

Figure 18

Wording for a Memorial Pamphlet
     For over (your number) years people have demonstrated their love and respect for others by making memorial contributions to (your institution). By this one generous act, they served the living and paid thoughtful tribute to the memory of a friend, associate, or loved one.

     If it is your decision to make such a gift, you may rest assured that it will be used by a system committed to providing the highest attainable (whatever) for the region we serve.

     An acknowledgement will be sent to the family of the person being honored. Your name and the purpose of the gift will be designated.

- The amount of your gift will not be disclosed.
- You will receive an official receipt for your tax-exempt gift.

Enclosed is a contribution of

$_____

In tribute to: _____

_____

Please send acknowledgement to:

Name _____

Address _____

From(your name) _____

Address _____
                (Please print legibly.)

125

Fund Raising 101

Chapter Twelve

Mail Fund Raising

If you keep in mind how important the acquisition of new donors is to the continued good health of your fund-raising effort, you will quickly learn that direct mail is one of the most frequently used methods of acquiring these badly needed donors.

If direct mail is new to you and your organization, then you will be happy to know that you need only learn three phases of fund raising by mail for your effort to be effective. These three phases are prospecting, mailing to previous donors, and testing. There are various names for these techniques, but by whatever name they are called there are basically only these three.

Prospecting

In prospecting, all you are doing is trying to locate those individuals who will give to your charity because they are motivated to do so by something sent to them through the mail from your organization.

Mailings to Previous Mail Donors

Once you have the names, addresses, and gift amounts from donors, they have qualified to be added to the previous-donor list.

Fund Raising 101

Right off the bat, we need to make you aware that raising money through the mail takes a long-term commitment by your organization. On top of that, it requires a significant cash outlay to get a mail program off the ground. However, fund raising by mail can produce profitable results and increase the number of donors entering the lower part of your pyramid.

Experts tell us that once prospects become donors, you may eventually write them six to ten times a year. Surprisingly, if you mail over and over to the same previous donor list, 13 percent will contribute each time you write.

The first time I worked with direct mail I was employed by the March of Dimes in Arkansas in the mid-1970s. At the time, I was wearing two hats: I was State Director and also the Director of The Central Arkansas Chapter, which consisted primarily of Little Rock and its surrounding suburbs. I provided supervision for two field representatives who worked the north and south halves of the state. Prior to these duties, I had been the field representative for the south half of the state, which was made up of seventy-five counties.

The March of Dimes was just beginning to take its mail program state-wide in the mid-1970s. It already existed in two or three chapters, but it was now being introduced in the smaller, less inhabited counties.

The mailing list had been purchased from a mail list house, and it contained all known addresses in the state. The early prospect mail pieces were addressed to "Dear Friend." In spite of the mailing package being a little primitive, the percentage returned were a little better then than they are today. Even the Dear Friend addresses returned as much as 3 percent. However, the gift size was smaller. I can remember thinking what a coup it was to get a $25 gift. A $50 or $100 gift had us in our cars going to the ends of the earth to meet the millionaire in person. To the best of my memory, we mailed our Dear Friend letters out only once annually. We made note of the name, any address correction, and the gift size of everyone who sent a gift back, regardless of size of the gift.

Mail Fund Raising

Sending out the mail to the previous donors was next. Now that we had a name, correct address, and gift size, we could mail directly to the giver. (See Figure 19.)

Figure 19

Mrs. A. B. Jones.
1234 Abby Lane
Kaytown, ST 76543
Dear Mrs. Jones,

Thank you for your gift of $5.00. The need is even greater this year, would you consider a gift of $7.00?

Ohhhh, that was big stuff back then! Our National Mail Team was telling us that many more people would increase their gift size by this attempt to upgrade their gifts than would be irritated by the request and not give at all. I was tough to convince but finally relented and accepted their word. They were right, mail giving increased, and that was what we were trying to accomplish.

In just two years we had increased the donors' giving level and frequency of giving. Many organizations that are heavily into mail today mail as much as twenty times annually to the same donor.

The use of mail has become a sophisticated technique. But you may not be there yet, and what I'm going to teach you in this chapter will take care of most of your immediate needs.

Before we move on, I should mention that you must pay attention to the effectiveness of your list, your letter, and the mailing package. The way to do this is to test. Write two or three test letters using a different style and language, and mail them to a group of one to two hundred of your list picked at random. Use a conversational, personalized writing style and don't be too wordy. Using long multisyllabic words is a curse. And always close with a postscript. Research tells us that more people read the postscript than any other part of the letter.

If you had a list of 25,000 names, you might pick every one-hundredth name and mail one of your letters. Duplicate this process with the other two test letters. Compile the results, and you have a pretty good idea of the kind and style of letter that your audience is most likely to respond to.

In another year you might want to test your package or turn-around document. Remember, a 1 or 2 percent improvement is money in the bank for years to come. Some serious mailers experiment with different sizes of envelopes. A No. 12 size is bound to grab the attention of the person opening the mail. However, a No. 10 envelope (the usual size used by businesses) is the most commonly used size.

Some of the Basic Principles

Not everyone is going to contribute to your organization by mail no matter how good the mail piece is. Just as people shop for a car by using different methods, they also prefer to contribute to charities in different ways.

I am a sucker for a child who comes to my door. I'm also a pretty easy mark at a roadblock when I can see the volunteers standing out in the hot sun or freezing rain. I'm not quite so easy at the door of a department store when someone is holding out a can. But I'm a pushover after I get inside the store and an employee is asking me for a donation on the store's time.

Well, those are the times when I'm easy. When am I not so easy? I rarely ever give through the mail. The only times that I have done so were to see what they would do with my name. Because I've always considered myself to be an average person, I have come to believe that most people feel as I do and have times when they will and when they won't give.

Next, let's explore what direct mail fund raising is and how it works. What is it? It is a single-letter attempt to move the prospect by your plea for a contribution to your organization. If you are to succeed, the letter must be compelling, using an economy of words. Let me give you a couple of examples of good and bad.

Examples:

BAD -- Our charity is responsible for more than 100,000 people who are now living independently.

GOOD - *Our charity has played an important role in teaching handicapped people how to adjust to the world around them. We're proud to have joined in this important effort that helped hundreds of handicapped individuals to take their rightful place in society.*

BAD -- Without your help, these handicapped adults will spend the rest of their lives sitting around watching television.

GOOD - *What a waste it would be, if allowed to continue, for these wonderfully creative people to have nothing better to do with their lives than to sit and watch TV. With your help and support, we can mobilize them in a constructive work program designed to maximize their potential.*

BAD -- Your gift will ensure that they will go to work very soon.

GOOD - *Our Adult Handicapped Rehab Program is just one of the many ways your contribution will go to work helping the people of our city.*

In addition to your "case" in an envelope, this is a good opportunity to provide the prospect with educational literature about your organization. Remember, try to include fund raising, friend raising, and education in everything you do.

Why Does Mail Work?

We have already addressed this question to a small degree. Some people prefer to support their charitable organizations through the mail. But why? Because many people, especially those confined to their homes, would have very few other opportunities if not for the United States Postal Service to feel worthwhile or to join with others

131

to remedy a problem. It's worth noting that mail donors are demonstrating their confidence in your institution by sending their money while knowing very little about its work.

How Do You Begin a Mail Program?

Start by analyzing your fiscal situation to determine if your organization can afford this expensive outlay of cash. Remember, mail will NOT add significantly to the revenue side of your ledger for a year or more. You will have to:

1. Invest in a prospecting mailer package.
2. Purchase, rent, or otherwise develop a prospect mailing list.
3. Process the contributions as they return.
4. Write thank-you letters.
5. Own and operate some sort of data record system so that you can send previous-donor pieces next time.

That's five steps and none of them without cost. The first, the prospecting mailer package, can be done by you or purchased from a professional mail producing house. The mail producing house can provide you with a turnkey product that will produce average results from the first time it's mailed. This is the direction that most people go and with justification. Those who decide to go on their own, more often than not invest time and money and usually have poor results.

The second step, a prospect mailing list, can often be provided by the charity that is about to embark on a mailing program. Hospitals have their patients, often referred to as a "grateful patient list." Colleges and universities have alumni and parents of alumni. The arts have names of the patrons of the symphony, theater, and museums.

However, after mailing to the obvious constituency, you can buy from list-selling businesses that sell lists by zip code, households with incomes over $50,000, and other categories. With today's technology, you can buy lists of almost any combination of categories—Democrats who subscribe to *Better Homes & Gardens* and drive Fords. The options are nearly limitless.

The third step is to process the contributions as they return, which requires time and manpower. Your staff must be sufficiently large to allow you to assign one person to open the returned mail, record the person's name, make any necessary corrections, and get a thank-you letter out by return mail. And of course, someone must prepare the bank deposit and enter the donors' names into a good system of record keeping.

The fourth step, although mentioned in step three, is writing a proper thank-you letter to the contributor. If you are computerized, and I hope that anyone who reads this book is, then you may have only to push a few buttons, and the proper thank-you will be printed. Someone then inserts it into the proper envelope and out it goes. If you are not computerized, this step is a big one. Someone will have to type a letter to each contributor, or you can have a generic letter printed. Either way, it must be done. Every next gift begins with the thank-you letter from the last gift.

The fifth step is to own and operate some sort of data record system so that you can send previous-donor pieces next time. Again, with a good computer record system, you can more easily control the education and involvement of your donors if you have adequate records of their giving history and their involvement with your charity. If you are going to try to upgrade donors' gifts in the future, it is imperative that you know what they gave in the past.

Writing Your Direct Mail Piece

Begin by analyzing your strengths. What makes your organization different from the others in your area? What is your organization's track record? Has it always been there in the time of community need? Are there some specific issues that will motivate people to contribute to your organization? Think through these questions carefully; be sure you have correct facts and data.

On the next page is an outline of the contents of an Appeal mail package:

Fund Raising 101

1. The outside envelope (the stamp, address labels or handwritten addresses, return address, and any teasers).
2. The appeal letter is usually one to four pages long. Most people feel that the shorter it is, the better.
3. The response mechanism, sometimes referred to as the reply document or turnaround document, is simply the piece that has the prospect's name, address, and suggested amount on it.
4. The reply envelope has your return address on it. It is commonly felt that if return postage is provided, it increases the number of returns. There are some organizations, however, that feel that anyone willing to contribute to their charity will not mind paying the postage.
5. Almost without exception, charities include an educational piece in all mailings. You will never have a better opportunity to have the educational piece read. The education piece should not be excessive in length; a page or two is acceptable.

You need to decide if you are going to do all this work in-house or hire professional consultants to develop your appeal package. Because there is so much diversity in this world and within the various organizations where I have consulted, I am hesitant to recommend the direction you should take.

If I were in a position where I wore many hats (for example, responsible for administration, fund raising, public relations, and sweeping up at night), I would hire it done by a pro. What I'm really saying is, do you have the time to do it right? If so, then do it. If not, then by all means get professionals in there and let them do it right from the beginning. If you botch it up in an unprofessional attempt to get a mail program off the ground, it will be harder and more costly to get the mess corrected later.

Let's assume that you have decided on the direction to go with your mailing piece. Your next decision is to determine how to get a mailing list. You can go the commercial route by purchasing, renting, or even trading for your list. Of course, you could compile it from various directories. Or maybe you are from an organization that has a good-sized list already, such as alumni, clients, donors, patients, friends, and so on.

There are no secrets to selecting your list--just some old fashioned, clear-headed thinking. If you have an alumni or patients list, it would be wise to begin to educate and massage the patient list before you start purchasing other lists. You can turn a patients list into a grateful patients list. There are colleges in the United States that have spent the time and energy to cultivate their alumni and as a reward many have a giving percentage of 50 to 60 percent, or more.

Smaller charities have the same opportunity. You simply have to decide who your constituency is and begin the process of communication, education, and involvement. Before you know it, you will have increased your donor pool.

Processing the Mail

You've done everything you're supposed to, and you are now at the point where the returns are beginning to come in. You must think about processing the gifts. I have a rule of thumb about sending acknowledgments. I want my acknowledgments or thank-you letters to be in the return mail within forty-eight hours. Remember, you start working on the
next gift with the thank-you from this one. So, be timely and grateful.

Any thank-you letter should include the following:

1. Start by thanking the donors and acknowledging their gifts.
2. Let the donors know that they have joined with other people who share their interest and generosity.
3. Describe the progress being made by your charity.
4. Describe how the donors and the community benefit. The following sentences are examples that you can adapt to your own use:
   a. Thank you for your generous gift to the ABC Foundation.

b.   By making this gift, you have joined with many other area donors in support of the Foundation's commitment to provide one of the finest "ABC ---" facility's possible.
c.   The generous support from you and you enabled the Foundation to make enormous progress over the last year.
d.   This with the benefits of a larger whatever, a deeperthing-ma-bob, and a taller what-ya-call-it. With the community's support, the ABC Organization will continue to provide the finest technology and the most highly skilled professionals available anywhere in the world.

By using these sample sentences as a start, you should be able to write a personal letter adapted to your own needs.

Donor Record System
We hope that you have a donor record-keeping system of some kind. If not, now is the time to begin. The simplest of donor records is a 4-by-8-inch or similar size index card. In the top left-hand corner put the first three initials of a donor's last name, followed by the first initial of the first name. Example: William L. Doyle becomes DOYW. Next comes the full name, place of employment, address, and phone number. And finally the pledge or gift amount. (See Figure 20.)

If you happen to be a large charity and you have a computer system, you must still keep the same type of information. However, you will code various types of mailings and enter them into your system accordingly.

Earlier in this chapter, we explained why mailing to prospects isn't a true fund-raising project. Fundamentally, it is a program for acquiring donors. Nonetheless, you must continually monitor the cost, but don't overcomplicate the process. Just be sure to keep up with all the costs, package design, and postage, and to estimate fairly the cost of the manpower involved. The combination of all these elements is your total cost.

Mail Fund Raising

Figure 20

DOYW

William L. Doyle	Office 876-9872
ABC Investment Company	Home 789-2001
987 North - 75th Street	
Anytown, US 39124	

Additional information can be kept on the front of the card like: wife's name, secretary's name, place of worship, college, and so on.
On the reverse side of the card you can keep the pledge/payment information.

Annual Campaign = 1, Door-to-door = 2, Black-tie event = 3, and so on.

Date	Pledge	Date	Paid	Balance	
12/25/91	$1,000	12/25/91	200	$ 800	1
		03/23/92	200	600	1
06/09/92	100	06/09/92	10	690	2
		08/19/92	190	500	1 & 2

Next, keep careful track of the revenue from the mail as it comes in. Subtract the expenses from the revenue. If you are plus or minus 1, 2, or 3 percent, you still have a winning donor acquisition program. Donor acquisition programs rarely make money; however, they are necessary if we are to have continued growth.

Half-Life Formula

The following is a formula for estimating the life cycle of your mailings. Each of your mailings will have what is referred to as a *half-life*. Half-life means that you have received about half of all the mail you will receive in total on the day that you receive your largest number of gifts. After that day, the number of gifts received each day begins to taper off.

Half-life averages:

* Local mailings: 12 to 14 days after you receive the first gift.

137

* Your state and surrounding states: 15 to 18 days after you receive the first gift.
* Nationally: 19 to 22 days after you receive the first gift.

Figure 21 is an actual example of a local mailing:

Figure 21   K E E P I N G   A   R E C O R D

M	T	W	T	F		M	T	W	T	F		M	T	W	T	F		M	T	W	T
Daily Gifts																					
0	0	0	3	5		17	9	10	15	14		23	16	12	9	7		15	10	8	8
Cumulative Gifts																					
0	0	0	3	8		25	34	44	59	73		96	16	28	37	44		59	69	77	85

Only five gifts were received after the twentieth day. This particular mailing was a prospecting piece and consisted of 19,240 names.

On the basis of what we have learned so far, would you think this mailing was successful or unsuccessful? See if you can figure it out. (This mailing produced a 0.098, just under 1 percent.)

Although the income from a prospect mailing is secondary, you might be curious to know what our net gain was—just over $1,300.

Odds and Ends

Be realistic in your expectations of your donors. You will harm your program if your expectations are unreasonably high.

Don't forget to factor in the labor and computer costs to get a complete picture of the total. In the foregoing example, labor was not figured into the results. With the labor, the mailing actually lost about $2,050.

Keep records that tell the length of time for the gifts to be returned. By doing so, you can more accurately predict returns.

Mail Fund Raising

You will rarely make a profit on prospect mailing; that's not its purpose. However, you will make it up in the future with previous-donor mailings.

Incorrect addresses and phone numbers on your prospect list are an unnecessary expense and will cost you extra money.

Annually, make an effort to purge your list, ridding it of incorrect names, addresses, and the like. Comb through your donor pool after every promotion. If you can afford to use them, there are list companies that for a fee can compare your donor pool with donors' information.

Experts tell us that a donors' response depends on the 40—40—20 Rule: 40 percent of response depends on list, 40 percent depends on your institution's mission, and the last 20 percent depends on the creativity of the mailing package.

Segmenting your list into zip codes is the easiest way to track your results when testing.

Proper evaluation of each mailing is imperative. I hope you have learned a little something about fund raising by mail. It's not complicated and it can be very rewarding. I have received letters from elderly men and women in shaky handwriting that brought me to tears. One of them enclosed two crumpled $1 bills and a note saying, "I wish I had more. They keep cutting my Social Security, but I want to help. I love my grandchildren."

Fund Raising 101

Chapter Thirteen

Special Events

Special events are used by most charities to raise funds and to have fun at the same time. In this chapter we cover some of the methods of doing that, and we remember the three major objectives of a fund-raising project: fund raising, friend raising, and education.

Special event fund raising is my favorite at least as much as capital campaigning. Special event fund raising allows everyone involved to be spontaneous and creative. Participants are limited only by their own imagination. If you are open and adventurous, you can try almost anything.

Some of my earliest special events were walk-a-thons, rock-a-thons, sit-a-thons, dance-a-thons, and about any other "a-thon" you can think of. Naturally, by cutting my teeth with a national charity, I was involved with door-to-door campaigns and other canvassing events. From "a-thons," I graduated to holiday favorites such as the House of Horrors and a New Year's Eve dance. Somewhere along the way I added jail and bail, ticket sales, black-tie events, and telethons.

I cannot honestly say that I have conducted every special event known to mankind, but I have been involved in many special events in many different forms. I have enough experience to know that along with the fun they are a lot of work. I have found that the money made in a special event is roughly equivalent to what you will have saved by not hiring employees to do the work. This seems hard to believe, but it's true. I have organized and conducted special events that have raised more than half a million dollars, and the profit was somewhere nearly equal to what I would have paid to hire employees to do the work. In addition, special events are generally felt to be the most expensive form of fund raising. Then why do them?

Simple! In addition to the money they raise, they provide an opportunity to activate your volunteers in meaningful service to your charity. Plus they are an excellent method for finding new volunteers and educating the public about your institution's services.

That's why!

Although special events are usually fun to conduct and they involve a lot of people, they still require careful planning. Without the planning, you and your group will meander all over the place trying to decide what comes next.

I use a standard format when I plan a special event. It is not perfect, but it is a good technique for organizing my thoughts.

Any Project

Start by writing a paragraph about what you are trying to accomplish. This is not the time for details, just a statement.

We want to create an event that the public will enjoy attending. Its <u>first</u> objective should be to raise money. The second object is to recruit and involve new volunteers. And the third is to provide some marketing and educational information about our institution. It is not necessary that every event have all three of the major objectives. It is important that you write down what you an event to achieve so that you can determine after it is over whether you have succeeded.

A More Specific Example

"A Chocolate Fantasy"

The object of the Chocolate Fantasy is to raise funds by organizing a party at which people who have purchased tickets can sample a wide variety of chocolate candies, pies, cakes, and any other concoctions that would tickle the fancy of any chocolate lover. The major objectives for this project are to raise funds, to recruit volunteers, and to provide education.

Planning:
- Recruit a chairman and various sub-chairs.
- Develop a plan, including estimated manpower, a time line, and a realistic budget.
- Sub-chairs recruit committee members.

Normal committees:
- Decorations
- Logistics
- Advertisement, promotions, and education
- Ticket sales
- Prizes
- Awards, thanks, and accounting
- Recruit and provide training for volunteers
- Identify the target audience to be reached

In addition to staff organizational responsibilities, their greatest value is in supporting the volunteers. Keep everyone on schedule and pointed in the right direction. The staff can do this by making sure that there is good communication among the volunteers and between themselves and the volunteers.

Special Events Accomplish All Three Major Objectives
They raise funds, friends, and educate.

First and foremost, special events raise funds, usually bringing donors in at the bottom of the pyramid. Of course, there are exceptions to this. Most black-tie occasions require a prospect to spend from $100 to $300 or more to gain entry. In the case of the black-tie event that we are currently conducting, the guests usually spend additional money purchasing silent and live auction items after they arrive.

Fund Raising 101

We have made a lot of friends for our hospital by conducting our black-tie event. For our event to work properly, it takes more than 100 volunteers each year. The need for so many volunteers has required the staff to assist in the recruiting and training of the volunteers. During the training and involvement process, these volunteers have become educated about our hospital and its many complex problems.

By describing a little about our black-tie event, I hope I have given you some idea about how special events are an excellent tool for accomplishing all three of our major objectives.

What to Charge

In special event fund raising, the cost of admission is often not quite so steep as for our black-tie event. Admission to a concert might be $15 or $20. Admission to a baseball card show could be $1 or $2. Naturally, the admission to any event varies depending on what the ticket holders receive for their investment and what the traffic is willing to pay.

One aspect of a special event that I am not too happy about is that the people who participate may not otherwise care about the charity; they are there only for the entertainment. Therefore, you need to be aware of this and work extra hard to use this opportunity to provide good education for them. It is not unusual for a charity to have a sign-up sheet readily available to get names for later use in mail solicitation. Do not assume that names gathered in this manner will be good and loyal supporters. You may have to work harder to educate them than you would people whose names you gathered in many other ways.

What Costs Are Reasonable

I have already mentioned that special events are one of the most expensive methods of raising money. Most fund-raising professionals feel that the cost of any special event should not exceed 35 percent of the gross income. However, that is a figure that you can shoot for. You may spend in excess of 100 percent to get

144

Special Events

a good special event started. If it is worth that to you and your organization, then do it.

I have already admitted to you that I have had some real turkeys in my fund-raising career. If the project is helping your organization reach other goals, don't let the cost frighten you away. If one of your objectives is to teach teens about the problems of teenage pregnancy, and if you are able to reach them through a rock-a-thon that might lose money, the cost could still be worth the loss.

Your Signature Event

Finding the right event for your charity can be very difficult. In the past five years, I have had the privilege of helping many of the charities in our area. This has been particularly gratifying to me because I have learned as much as I have taught. I have discovered that everyone wants to own a special event that is synonymous with the charity they support. That would be possible if every charity would take on the risk and the workload that comes with owning an event. As I mentioned earlier in this chapter, the profit made from a special event is usually about equal to the value of the work expended by the charity's volunteers.

I was recently invited to talk with a local service club about fund raising. I told them what I have just written here. If they wanted to make money for their club's treasury, the profit would be about equal to the work expended by their clubs members.

They may have been the first group to believe me. At least, the project they chose as their signature project reflected their willingness to work for the profit. They decided to gather and sell winter firewood to anyone in the community who wished to purchase it. A local land owner donated any fallen timber on his land and each service club member was asked to volunteer a minimum of ten hours. During their hours they could chop the firewood or they could haul and stack it at the purchasers' homes. If work, family, or medical reasons prevented them from participating, they could opt out for $10 an hour, $100.

Fund Raising 101

When the project ended, they had chopped, hauled, and stacked $3,295 worth of firewood. They collected $2,590 from members who had opted out. Their expenses were about $1,320, leaving a profit of $4,565. Someone told me that the resulting profit was about $2.10 per man hour. Due to the tremendous hard work with this project, they have decided that this event will not become their signature event.

At our foundation we have three signature events. Each one requires immense time and effort. I've already mentioned that we conduct a black-tie event. It is called the Three Star Gala. Ninety to 100 volunteers participate in this event each year. The Three Star Gala occurs each year in early November. We have our first meeting for the next year before the end of November. It is a year-round project that raises about $500,000.

The gala's organization consists of an overall chair person and the normal offices, plus eight sub-committee chairs. The event also has a vice-chair who recruits the sub-committee vice-chairs during her year as vice-chair. (The leadership of the Gala has always been women.) Using this method, all of next year's sub-committee chairs are being trained during the current year. It makes for a smooth transition. Every chair and vice-chair has a job description for their responsibility. They also have goals that are established during the evaluation meeting that takes place the week following the gala.

One of the things that makes our gala unique is its cost. We do not come near the 35 percent that is considered average. Our gala costs rarely exceed 15 percent.

Two other signature events for our foundation are the annual telethon and the rubber duck race.

We are fortunate to be one of the 160 member hospitals associated with the Children's Miracle Network Telethon. We use the Telethon as an umbrella event during which we can report on most of our other special events. We conduct about twenty-five special events each year. Most of them are small events that bring in from a few hundred to a few thousand dollars. Four events among the twenty-five are fairly large. The Balloon Hang-ups raise around $75,000, the Phon-a-thon raises about $35,000, an individual solicitation (called the Advance Gifts Division) raises about $40,000, and an employee project raises about $50,000. The rest are smaller events.

The final signature event for us is the Rubber Duck Race. We have other larger events, but the community really likes the duck race. Last year we began to talk about the possibility of replacing the Rubber Duck Race with something a little less laborious. The Chamber of Commerce got wind of our discussions and asked us to reconsider. They liked the event because it involves thousands of people in a wholesome family-style, outside event. We begin the day at 8:00 A.M. with a sanctioned 5-kilometer run. At 9:00 A.M. there is a fitness walk for all ages. At 11:00 A.M. about 2,000 children show up, with their parents in tow, for the Easter "Duck" Egg Hunt. Next comes a variety of activities for the entire family including games, music, and food. At 1:20 P.M., 10,000 rubber ducks dive off the overpass and swim like crazy trying to help their adopted parents win a million dollars.

In case I've confused you, we have three signature events, the Three Star Gala, the Telethon, and the Rubber Duck Race. These events are known by the community to be associated with our hospital.

Profit

It is important that you keep a careful analysis of the cost per each dollar raised. And be sure to include the costs of staff time in the budget. It is essential for determining the profitability of your event. And do not overlook the number of volunteer man hours. If you have a handle on this information, you can make an informed decision about whether or not to include a particular project in your annual plan for the next year.

What You Can Learn from Special Events

Special events are a marvelous cultivation tool for new

prospects as well as being a good vehicle for involving some of your current donors. While reviewing some of our hospital's donors recently, I noticed a $1,000 gift in each of the past three years from the same woman. I called to thank her for the continued support of our children's program. As we talked, I discovered that she had a son who was suffering from muscular dystrophy. Knowing this about her helped me to understand how I could help her get involved in our charity.

Conducting a special event is often the preferred method for determining new volunteers' level of interest because it introduces them to your institution. Special events also provide excellent opportunities for new volunteers to socialize with current members of your charity's "family."

Types of Special Events

There are as many special events as there are people. The following is a list of special events that I have divided into two value categories: high dollar and low dollar.

High-dollar special events (events with the potential to raise thousands of dollars)

Black-Tie Dinners	Walk-A-thons
Auctions	Lotteries
Duck Race	Coin Canisters and Kites
Hands On	Wine Tasting
Bike-a-thon	Food Fair
Horse Shows	Murder Mystery
Outstanding Citizen Party	Radio Days
Jail-and-Bail	Tribute Dinners
Derby Party	$100 Club
Scavenger Hunt	

Low-dollar special events (events with the potential to raise hundreds of dollars)

Ads at your events	Bake Sales
Baseball Card Show	Brick Sale
Concessions	Cow Patty Bingo

Special Events

Guess Jelly Beans   Used Book Sale
Happy Tree   Soft Drink Sale
Lock and Key Sale   Mini Fair
Movie fund raisers   Paint Curb Numbers
Pancake Breakfast   Penny a Vote
Phantom Party   Quarter Carnival
Red Stocking Follies
Helium Balloons w/numbers inside
General Store/Similar to garage sale
Theater Party w/Santa Claus/Candy in Bags
Travel Agency (points for buying tickets)

I am sure that someone could take a low-dollar event and make several thousand dollars with it, and the opposite could be true with some of the high-dollar events. I just wanted to provide you with a list of events in which I have participated and the results we received. Any event will be improved if the planning is good and volunteer involvement and determination are strong.

Where to Begin with a Special Event

Select a special event about which your staff and volunteers can get excited. Recruit a chairperson and planning committee. Develop a realistic budget and time line, and you are on your way.

Following are two projects for which the planned outline has already been developed. They will give you an idea of the organization that you will need in any project that you undertake. The two projects are old standbys: A Tribute Dinner and a Rock-a-thon.

In Your Honor — A Tribute Dinner

The object of the event is to raise funds by having guests gather to honor someone they respect. The guests pay more for the dinner tickets than the cost of the meal (and other activities). Why a dinner? A dinner is often less expensive than many other special events. All you need is a deserving individual, a good meal, maybe some entertainment, and a few miscellaneous items, mostly donated.

Tribute dinners give your charity the opportunity to educate those in attendance about your cause as well as honor an outstanding person.

Phase One: The Planning Phase
1. Select a very important, influential person to be the chairperson. The Steering Committee should be made up of the Steering Committee chairperson and the chairperson of each of the sub-committees, plus three at-large members. The Steering Committee should retain the right to veto or change the decision of a sub-committee, but it should do so only when necessary. It should approve all important decisions: the person to be honored, the program for the evening, the budget, whether or not to serve alcoholic beverages, and so on.
2. Select an individual who is deserving and is likely to accept this recognition. <u>It is very helpful if this individual has a following.</u> The honoree should be a man or woman of such influence that many people will <u>want</u> to attend.
3. The Steering Committee should develop the program and script for the evening. Assigning an amount of time for each activity and speaker is good planning. Allowing only three minutes for this and two minutes for that will cause everyone to pre-plan.

Recommended Sub-Committees
a. Honoree Selection Committee
b. Invitation/Ticket/Accounting Committee
c. Logistics Committee
d. Publicity Committee
e. "Thank You" Committee

Phase Two: The Pre-event Activities
1. The Honoree Selection Committee should develop a pool

Special Events

consisting of names of individuals who deserve to be honored. It should rate the persons on whether they deserve an honor of this magnitude, whether people would want to see any of these individuals honored, and whether these persons' personas are harmonious with your charity's cause.

2 The Invitation/Ticket/Accounting Committee should develop a pool of names of individuals who may wish to attend the tribute. Seek suggestions from the honoree, who will realize that his or her name and reputation are being used to aid a very important charity in the community. Therefore, the honoree is usually very willing to furnish names for you to invite.

Do not overlook civic organizations that your honoree is involved in as well as place of worship, work, college, and the like.

If the honoree is important enough, businesses such as the gas, electric, and phone companies, banks, and manufacturing companies will wish to be included.

3. The Logistics Committee is responsible for the following on the dinner night:
- parking
- where to seat the people as they arrive
- a short but interesting program
- what to do with the honoree and his or her personal guests prior to the event
- arrival and seating of paid guests
- head table seating
- food selection
- method of serving
- whether or not to have alcoholic beverages

4. The Publicity Committee is responsible for getting newspaper coverage for the announcement of the honoree, the announcement of any special guests, and coverage of the actual event. It may be appropriate to have a newsletter to send to those involved to keep them informed.

151

Fund Raising 101

Phase Three: Conducting the Event
1. Appoint someone to be in charge of the evening. Pre-check the microphone system, lights, layout of the room, and table settings, and make sure the number of servers is adequate.

Phase Four: Thanking and Accounting

1. The "thank-you" committee is responsible for thanking those who bought tickets or donated prizes or awards, or those merchants who provided support.
2. Make a public accounting of how much money was raised and how it is to be spent to reinforce the giving habit.

* * * * * * * * * *

Rock-a-Round-the-Clock

The object of this event is to raise funds by recruiting people of all ages to do the following:

a. Secure sponsors for themselves who pledge cents or dollars per hour.
b. Commit to rocking in a rocking chair for twenty-four hours at a prescribed location, and
c. Collect the pledges from their sponsors and turn them in to your charity.

Businesses that cater to young people or sell products that would be featured in a Rock-a-Round-the-Clock should be sought for co-sponsorship. Examples include a local furniture store, radio station, fast food franchise, to name a few.

Rockers secure as many pledges as possible from sponsors. Each sponsor signs the sponsor form, pledging to make a specific gift — for example, 0.50, $1, $5 — to your cause for each hour the rocker rocks. Next the rockers rock in the event; your charity documents how many hours they rock; then the rockers go back to

152

their sponsors and collect the pledged amounts. Finally, the rockers turn the money over to your charity.

> Example: Rocker No. 1 secures the following pledges:
>
> | | |
> |---|---|
> | Joe Jones | $1.00 per hour |
> | Franie Hughes | 0.25 per hour |
> | Bob Jones | 5.00 per hour |
>
> Total pledges of $9.50 × 20 hours = $190

If you have 50 rockers who average $190 each, they will have earned $9,500 for your cause.

Conducting a Rock-a-Round-the-Clock can involve a few people, dozens of people, even hundreds. Volunteers of all kinds will be needed. Involve men, women, teenagers, and children to assist you in raising funds for your cause. (Minors will need their parents written permission to participate.)

This type of event can attract the attention of a wide range of people. Youngsters can secure sponsors from their doctors, teachers, friends, parents, and neighbors. These sponsors can afford to make generous gifts, and they may even become first-time donors to your cause because a rocker asked them for support.

Besides youngsters this event may include oldsters, disabled people in wheelchairs, single parents, couples, and teams from various clubs and or work places. I have seen people participating in this event who were 75 years old and 11 years old, as few as five people and as many as 150. I have seen this event raise $500 and $7,500. I have seen sponsor sheets with $1 in pledges and $1,100 in pledges. Your organization can make as much or as little as you choose. It's up to you!

Phase One: The Planning Phase
1. Select a chairperson and a vice-chairperson (to provide continuity for next year), and recruit a steering committee. The Steering Committee is made up of the Steering Committee chairperson and the chairperson of each of the

sub-committees, plus three at-large members. The Steering Committee retains the right to veto or change the decision of a sub-committee but only when necessary. The Steering Committee approves all important decisions, such as the grand prize, the date for the event, the appropriate sub-committees, the budget, and so forth.

2.   Recommend sub-committees and recruit the chairperson.

Sub-committees

a. Rockers Committee

b. Prize Gathering Committee

c. Public Relations Committee

d. Logistics Committee

e. Awards, Thanking, and Accounting Committee

Phase Two: The Pre-event Activities

1.   The Rockers Committee is responsible for the recruitment and coordination of the rocking participants. One person keeps track of and is responsible for mailing instructions and sponsor sheets to all the rockers before the event.

Where does the committee find rockers?

- schools
- Sunday School classes
- teen clubs
- boys' and girls' clubs
- Ys

Where do the rockers find sponsors?

- parents and grandparents
- door-to-door in most neighborhoods
- friends and classmates
- local businesses, doctors and dentists

NOTE: When rockers are out looking for sponsors, they should be clearly identified by a large name tag, with a phone number that can be called to identify them. (See Figure 22.)

Notify your local police department that you will have solicitors out during a certain period.

2. The Prize Gathering Committee is responsible for gathering the prizes. Prizes provide the incentive needed to encourage people of all ages to spend their time gathering sponsors and rocking in their rockers for twenty-four hours.

Figure 22
The wearer of this badge is a participant in the 1995 Rock-a-Round-the-Clock for Mid-Town Service Club Call 234-5678 for verification

Local merchants are usually very generous about providing prizes in the $5 to $25 range, such as dinners for two, a free pass at a local spa, and movie passes. Major prizes such as airline tickets to New Orleans or Hawaii are sometimes available to some charities.

3. The PR Committee is responsible for getting the word out to the newspapers and radio and TV stations. Recruiting a popular radio station to become a co-sponsor of Rock-a-Round-the-Clock usually pays dividends.

4. The Logistics Committee is responsible for the following:
   - Securing a location for Rock-a-Round-the-Clock (for example, an automobile dealer's showroom or a mall).
   - Providing water and other refreshments (fruit, soft drinks, snacks, for example).
   - Providing volunteers to help on the day of Rock-a-Round-the-Clock.
   - Coordinating the equipment needed by volunteers: rocking chairs, tables, chairs, calculators.
   - Arranging for rest rooms.
   - Arranging for a timekeeper (participants rock for 50 minutes with a 10 minute break each hour).
   - Providing some form of entertainment.

Fund Raising 101

Phase Three: Conducting the Event

All the workers show up early. A registration table will already have been arranged for, the rocking chairs are in place, the timekeeper is ready, refreshments are available, the participants show up, and Rock-a-Round-the-Clock officially begins.

Before you know it, Rock-a-Round-the Clock is over and the cleaning crew is doing their job.

Phase Four: Awards, Thanking, and Accounting
1. The Awards Committee prepares for an awards ceremony that could include a thank-you party.
2. The thank-you Letters Committee makes sure everyone who deserves gratitude receives it. Appropriate receipts are included with the thank-you letters to the merchants, the volunteers, the media, the rockers, and all others concerned. For a typical thank-you letter, see Figure 23.
3. The Accounting Committee makes every effort to collect the pledges from the sponsors. Your charity has at least three options for collecting the funds:
    a. To rely on the rockers to collect the pledges in advance. They can do this by asking the pledging parties to contribute a flat fee in advance.
    b. Ask the rockers to go back to the sponsors afterward to collect the pledges.
    c. Mail a statement directly to the sponsors. This is the method I recommend.

The sponsor sheet shown in Figure 24 can be used for almost any a-thon event.

Special Events

Figure 23

January 28, 1994

Mr. John Q. Public
1234 Next Street
Anytown, KS 98765-4321
Dear Mr. Public:

　　　　Your support, along with that of the other 165 sponsors, caused Rock-a-Round-the-Clock to be both a social and a financial success. Twenty-seven local merchants participated in this event. More than forty-seven rockers completed the twenty-four hours, and another twenty-seven rocked most of the hours.

　　　　I hope you are as excited as we were to learn that Mid-Town Service Club raised $7,950. This money will be used to supplement heating bills this winter, provide a nice Christmas for some underprivileged children, and provide training for our next year's club president. These activities would not be possible without your generosity.

　　　　Let me thank you again on behalf of the Mid-Town Service Club. A receipt is enclosed for your convenience.

Sincerely,

Billy Brown, Chairperson
Mid-Town Service Club's Annual Rock-a-Round-the-Clock

Figure 24
                         Rock for
Those Who Can't
for Mid-Town Service Club
Call 234-5678

Sponsor _____

Address_____

Amount Per Kilometer_____

1.
2.
3.
4.
5.
6.
7.
8.
9.
10.
11.
12.
13.
14.
15.
16.
17.
18.
19.   TOTAL

Chapter Fourteen

Planned Giving

A planned gift is
> **Any gift for any amount, given for any purpose...**
> **operations, capital expansion or endowment...**
> **whether for current or deferred use,**
> **if the assistance of a professional staff person,**
> **a qualified volunteer, or the donor's advisors**
> **is necessary to complete the gift.**
> **In addition, it includes any gift which is**
> **carefully considered by a donor,**
> **in light of the individual's estate**
> **and total financial plan.**
> **Robert F. Sharpe**

Planned Giving Made Easy

One of the aspects of the fund-raising profession that I enjoy most is helping smaller charities understand and conduct fund-raising programs and projects. In my desire to help them, I have come to understand that I have to keep things simple. The reason is that people working in the smaller charities have to perform many different jobs at the same time. Most small charities just can't afford the time and money to send their executive director away for training in all aspects of fund raising. In this chapter, I am directing the information toward the people who want to know enough about planned giving to include it in their programs without having to devote their lives to learning all there is to know.

I have attempted to make planned giving simple. There is no reason why every single individual who has fund raising as a responsibility can't go out and function in planned giving after reading this chapter.

Understanding how planned giving works, the legalese involved, the tax ramifications, the laws; none of this is easy. But the job of the professional fund raiser IS easy.

Before I explain what we do, I must acknowledge one of the very few people in the entire world whom I consider a mentor. Robert F. Sharpe is that for me. I attended his eight seminars a few years ago, and I came away awestruck by this man. I know only one other person who is his equal in the classroom.

Bob Sharpe has a natural talent for telling the story of how planned giving works. He is the first to tell you that you don't have to be a lawyer or an accountant or any other of the professionals normally associated with planned giving. All you have to do is be patient and polite and calmly work through the four Ps: People, Property, Plan, and Professionals.

A prospect for planned giving must have certain characteristics if you are to secure a gift. The prospect should have some wealth (although a gift of $5,000 or $10,000 is worth considerable effort). Another aspect is that of age. Seniors benefit the most from planned giving, but there are certainly opportunities to promote planned giving to individuals in their forties and fifties.

This is the scenario. If you have a prospect who is interested in contributing to your charity, your job is to promote an interview with this individual. Let's suppose the individual we are discussing is a seventy-four-year-old woman. Ask for an appointment, and with good luck, you are invited to Mrs. Jone's home.

You arrive at the appointed time, and Mrs. Jones is waiting for you with milk and cookies. This wouldn't be at all unusual. Many seventy-four-year-old women and men have few opportunities for company and often go to extremes to make their guests comfortable.

The conversation might begin by your asking Mrs. Jones how long she has been a resident of Anytown. Where did she grow up? What did her parents do for a living when she was a young. Did she marry and to whom? What did she and her husband do for employment during their lifetimes? Does she have children? What do the children do now that they are grown up? Are there any grandchildren? What are her hobbies and interest?

No doubt, you are getting the idea.

From this line of conversation, with subtle questioning, Mrs. Jones is going to tell you the financial status of her parents, whether she inherited anything, what her husband did, and whether they were able to amass wealth. Your asking about her marriage and life makes it likely that she will tell you much about her property. Asking about her children and hobbies will probably cause her to tell you much of what are likely to be her plans for her children and friends. With only a little coaxing, you should easily draw out her plans for her place of worship or charities that interest her.

If you have been taking good notes, you can summarize the things she has related to you. You might say something like, "*Mrs. Jones, let me see if I have your thoughts and plans properly outlined. I think you said that you have this house, another in the country, and that you own a farm that you rent out in Oklahoma. I think you indicated that you don't owe anything on these properties and that you have an income of approximately $800 a month from the rental of these properties. I think you mentioned that you have some CDs in the bank that are valued at about $100,000. You have a car that is paid for and miscellaneous jewelry valued at about $20,000.*" You may have to guess at a couple of these things in the hope that she will correct you for accuracy.

You go on with, "*I think you indicated that both of your children are very well situated financially, so you want to leave the bulk of your estate to your grandchildren for their education. You mentioned a few friends with whom you socialize. Do you wish to include them in your estate planning?"* She may indicate yes or no. Record whatever she says. Although she may have mentioned her place of worship or charities earlier, you may still have to ask to be certain. *"Mrs. Jones, do you have any intention to include your church or the ABC Charity in your estate planning?"* Record whatever the answer is.

You are nearly finished. You may have been with Mrs. Jones for several hours. I've heard of instances when this process went on for many visits adding up to twenty, thirty, or more hours. Patience and an enjoyment of history are marvelous assets for both the novice and the senior professional fund raiser in conducting the four Ps with a prospect. You may go all the way through the Ps only to find that the prospect may not have any interest in contributing to your organization. Worse yet, she may not want to do anything about her estate planning. So, if you have a love of mankind, you will enjoy this work a little more.

Now you are in the home stretch. You have a good list of her property, people, and her plan. Now all you need are her professionals. *"Mrs. Jones, who is your estate planning attorney? Do you have a CPA?"* Her next door neighbor may be a trial lawyer and she mentions his name. To some people a lawyer is a lawyer; they may not be aware that attorneys often specialize in certain aspects of the law. Point out that she probably wouldn't want a podiatrist performing brain surgery on her. Tell her that attorneys also specialize. For now, we will assume that she has an attorney with terrific experience in estate planning and that she or he has steered her to a CPA with similar experience. The prospect gives you their names.

You thank her for her courtesy and return to your office to organize your notes into logical steps. You provide a copy of this document to the prospect, her attorney, and her CPA. You are within bounds to offer to meet with anyone she chooses to explain your notes if she wishes you to. This does happen occasionally but not very often.

Planned Giving

At this point, you have done all you can do. Did I mention a charitable remainder uni-trust with replacement for the family? A bargain sale? A charitable lead trust? No, I didn't. The reason is that as fund raisers, we are acting unprofessionally if we place ourselves in a position that might be construed as making suggestions to prospects concerning the various instruments available in planned giving.

The more you know about planned giving, the more value you can be to your organization and to the prospects. I'm in favor of knowing all I can about the practice of planned giving. I just want you to know that you can make wonderful things happen for your charity without being all that knowledgeable. I get a little tired of some of my peers who know something that I don't and somehow want me to be in awe of their great wisdom. If I am going to be in awe of anyone, it's going to be someone like Bob Sharpe. He's earned it.

Planned Giving Instruments for Deferred Giving

The most commonly used instruments for deferred giving are bequests. Many senior fund raisers will tell you that if you have limited resources put them all into the process of securing bequests. Why? Because of all planned gifts received each year, bequests represent over 90 percent. For some reason, uni-trusts, lead-trusts, and the like receive more attention than bequests do. Yet, most charities receive the greatest part of their planned giving income from the bequest. Many senior fund raisers will tell you that if you have limited time and money for planned giving, put it into a bequest programs. They produce greater rewards.

Other types of planned gifts are summarized as follows:
-- Various Trusts
    > Charitable lead
    > Charitable remainder
    > Annuity trusts
    > Deferred payment annuities
    > Pooled income funds

-- Life Insurance
-- Retirement Plans
-- Revocable Living Trusts
-- Life Estate Agreements
-- Gifts of property, including
  > Real estate
  > Leases and Mortgages
  > Art
  > Patents and Royalties
  > IRAs and retirement plans
  > Stock and other property

Some Interesting Facts About Planned Giving

Planned giving is growing in its importance because people are living longer. Approximately 400,000 people retire annually, creating more opportunities than ever before for individuals to give to charity by using insurance, various trusts, and bequests.

The success of many charities will depend on the knowledge and techniques developed in promoting and managing planned giving. This knowledge will be shared by the professionals as well as the volunteers. With proper organization, your charity can recruit a professional advisory committee made up of attorneys, CPAs, CLUs, and trust officers of banks. With a group of these professionals, any question you could possibly need an answer to should be easily researched.

Most fund raisers understand that we must always put the prospect's real interest first. I sometimes say that the first 10,000 considerations in planned giving are all <u>what's good for the donor</u>. A planned giving professional's only consideration is how a plan can best serve the needs of the donor. If you go into any planned giving situation with this as your credo, you will get more than your fair share of planned gifts for your charity. Anything less, and I can't be proud of you.

Planned Giving

Getting a Planned Giving Program Started

If people who are new in the profession understood how little they need to know to get started, they wouldn't be so worried about planned giving. You can get your program up and running very nicely if you develop the following:

- A professional advisory committee.
- A planned giving development committee.
- Policies concerning the types of gifts your charity will seek.
- Policies for accepting gifts.

And know the 4 Ps (People, Property, Plans, and Professionals).

Start Your Planned Giving Program with Bequests

As has already been mentioned, bequests are by far the easiest planned gift to promote, yet they are usually large when compared to a small charity's operating budget. It's relatively easy to promote bequests. Following are a few things you can do:

☞ Identify a group of twenty-five, fifty, or a hundred of your most likely prospects, and begin an orderly communication with them about planned giving opportunities. If you don't have time or expertise in writing such communications, there are many very good newsletters available that will meet your needs. (Check fund-raising tradepapers like the Chronicle of Philanthropy or NonProfit Times for names of companies who sell them.)

☞ Suggest to members of your professional advisory committee that they include your targeted group of prospects in any mailing that they do to their preferred customers. The targeted group could be invited to seminars that the professionals conduct from time to time.

☞ Be sure to include thought-provoking comments in your mailing—for example, reminders about the importance of making a will, and the opportunity a will gives to benefit others, both members of their family and the ABC Charity.

☞ Initiate a planned giving club. You could call it the Legacy Club, Heritage Club, or Cornerstone Club, whatever you

165

think sounds right for your organization. To become members, individuals have only to make you aware that they have included your charity in their will. It's not important that you know the amount, just that they have done it.

☞ Be sure to make a planned gift yourself and ask your Board to do likewise.

☞ Make a fuss over individuals who make a planned gift. It's not even important that they did it for your organization. By promoting planned giving, regardless of who gets the gift, you will be teaching planned giving in your community. Your charity will get a fair share.

☞ Promote and conduct a Wills Week. You can do this by asking your local paper to join you in the promotion. They are usually willing to do so as soon as they find out the positive impact a wills week can have. Also, ask a bank to sponsor the wills week. If you have a Ministers' Alliance in your community, they will usually be happy to join your effort.

The forgoing list contains a few of the things you can do to give your planned giving program some visibility. If you do all or most of these things, you will become a leader in your community in planned giving. And once again, I want to point out that you can do these things knowing hardly anything about the various planned giving instruments.

One more thing about bequests before I move on. It is commonly felt that only 31 percent of Americans have wills at the time of their death. And 69 percent of those who do, have the simple "I love you" or "sweetheart" will that leaves everything to their spouse.

Simple Policies on Accepting Gifts Other than Cash

I have seen and been a party to some very complicated policies concerning accepting charitable gifts. On occasion they

166

Planned Giving

made sense. However, the following simple policies work very nicely in most organizations.

1. The development office encourages the giving of any noncash asset if it can either be used by some unit of the institution or if it can be sold for cash within a reasonable time.

2. No item will be accepted if it is encumbered by debt or if the use of, or cash received from, the sale of the property is restricted by race, religion, age, or sex.

3. The donor will be responsible for establishing the value of the gifted property.

4. The chief development officer, with the concurrence of the chairman, is authorized to accept or reject any noncash gift. If these two individuals cannot agree on acceptance or rejection of the proposed gift, the decision should be made by the organization's executive committee.

5. The sale of the gifted property that cannot be used by the institution will be accomplished as soon as possible for cash. The chief development officer, with the help of anyone he or she selects from the executive committee, will be responsible for the sale.

Starting a Planned Giving Program

-   Create a plan that outlines your activities for at least three years.
-   Gain complete buy-in by the board.
-   The board must commit the necessary financial resources.
-   Working together, the board and staff establish policies.
-   The board cultivates prospects and actively recruits gifts.
-   Assign responsibilities.

The staff has responsibility for the following:

-   Obtaining the technical knowledge needed to operate a planned giving program.
-   Knowing the best use of volunteers.
-   Knowing where to go for legal advice.

Fund Raising 101

- Locating the legal and reporting requirements (The Professional Advisory Committee is the source).
- Developing a minimum understanding of the various planned giving instruments.
- Developing calling techniques, including listening and fact-gathering skills (the 4 Ps).
- Participating in various training opportunities by attending the appropriate seminars, reading the available publications, and getting involved with local support or networking groups.
- Understanding that the prospects' interests and protection of their wealth is the staff's first concern.
- Working hard and being a good cheerleader for the program.
- Drafting policy statement.
- Seeking advice and together constructing a solid plan for the charity.
- Recruiting, training, and involving a professional advisory committee and door-opening committee.
- Providing regular evaluation.

The board has responsibility for the following:
- What types of planned giving instruments will be available.
- Investment policies and guidelines.
- Rates to be paid.
- Who makes investment decisions.
- How the money is spent.
- What will be the minimum needed for each instrument.
- Who is authorized to negotiate for gifts.
- Confidential information--precautions.
- Authorization for negotiation with donor.
- Tax requirements (knowledge of IRS forms 8282 and 8283).
- A continuing responsibility for developing prospects and opening doors for the planned giving officer.

Planned Giving

More About a Professional Advisory Committee
A professional advisory committee can do the following:
- Provide technical advice on your written materials.
- Write technical articles for your in-house publications or local newspapers.
- Put on all types of planned giving seminars.
- Open doors to good prospects.
- Recommend your institution to their clients when a charitable gift is in order.

More About a Planned Giving Development Committee
This committee should be made up of people who are willing to use their connections and influence to open doors and get for the development officer appointments with prospects.

Marketing Your Planned Giving Program
What do you want to accomplish in marketing your planned giving program?
- Gain high visibility for your program.
- Positioning--try to establish your program as the premier program in the area.
- Meet people who could benefit by your program.
- Publicize that your charity is providing this service.
- Secure planned gifts.

How to Gain High Visibility
- Determine your constituency and begin a direct mail program providing them with timely informational materials (I mentioned doing this earlier with only twenty-five people. The larger the list the better).
- Have your most prestigious leaders write personal letters to them .
- Secure underwriting from banks and other appropriate sources to pay for advertisements.
- Advertise in all your institution's publications.

Fund Raising 101

How Do You Find Personal Contacts?

- Public seminars
- CPAs' offices
- Real estate offices
- Will clinics
- Personal contacts

- Banks
- Attorneys' offices
- Professional seminars
- Estate planning seminars
- Estate planning councils

I hope you agree that we have taken some of the mystery out of planned giving, making it easier to understand and to practice. I realize that I have drastically simplified the process. The reason I have done so is not to minimize the work of planned giving officers who have worked so hard to hone their skills. To the contrary, I just want you to stop being concerned about what you don't know and put to work the many skills that you do know. If you attempt to activate your planned giving program in the ways that I have suggested, in no time you will be talking about the planned giving instruments with the rest of the pros.

Chapter Fifteen

Capital Campaigning

Capital campaigning is the method most often used by charities to fund capital expansion. Examples include the following: a new hospital, an addition to a hospital, an expensive piece of equipment, a new building for a college, a new building for a performing arts center, renovation of a museum, and so on. The list is quite extensive and often includes endowment.

It is generally agreed that the capital campaign process should evolve naturally from the strategic plan of the institution. It is also agreed that for a capital campaign to achieve its greatest potential the campaigning charity must have earned the support it is seeking.

Earning Support

Support can be earned in various ways. For example; the existence of a popular museum in a community brings additional traffic for local businesses. Therefore, the local business community has a stake in the success or failure of the museum. Should the museum go out of existence, the local businesses would suffer a loss of income as a result of the loss of the extra traffic.

Let me give you an example in which I was personally involved. While working for Community Service Bureau, a capital campaign consulting company, I was assigned to organize a campaign for Tougaloo College, a small southern black college in

Fund Raising 101

Jackson, Mississippi. The feasibility study had been carried out by a co-worker. I came in for the planning and solicitation phases.

Tougaloo began during the late 1800s and was well known as an excellent school for the black population of Mississippi. As segregation began to pass into history, many well-educated black men and women had graduated from Tougaloo and hat taken their places in education and business throughout Mississippi.

During the feasibility study, many of the white leaders of Jackson stepped forward without the slightest hesitation in support of Tougaloo College. Their response to the questions in the feasibility was, "*Tougaloo has been a good corporate citizen; I will be delighted to work in the campaign.*"

When the president and CEO of what was the largest banking institution in the state at that time was asked to chair the campaign, his answer was, "*Absolutely, Tougaloo has always been there for the black population, now it's there for black and white. They have never asked for anything from us, it's about time we gave them a hand.*"

I was impressed by his answer, and throughout the campaign, I heard these types of statements repeated over and over. Tougaloo had earned the respect of the business community by their good citizenship, and the business community was ready and willing to return the favor. The campaign was an easy winner.

This is what I am referring to when I say that a charitable organization needs to earn or deserve support. There are far too many charities that seem to feel as though the community owes them success simply because they are a charity. **Well, it ain't necessarily so!**

The Phases of a Capital Campaign
A capital campaign includes three phases:
1. Feasibility study
2. Planning
3. Solicitation

172

Capital Campaigning

Having conducted six campaigns, I can tell you from personal experience that planning and conducting the campaign is many times more difficult if you did not personally conduct the preceding feasibility study. You get information in the study that can't be written down. For example, during the questioning process, the person being interviewed can sometimes say with body language something different from what he or she is telling you.

Many charities, in an effort to save money, decide to pass up the feasibility study. That would never happen with any charity that I am involved with. When this happens, I am immediately reminded of the saying, *"penny wise, pound foolish."* The feasibility study is designed to tell you seven things:

1. The individuals that will give personal financial support.
2. The corporations that will give financial support.
3. The people who should be asked to be leaders in the campaign.
4. If there are enough people willing to work as solicitors in the campaign.
5. If the timing is correct for the campaign.
6. It tests your case with the community.
7. It identifies your charity's strengths and weaknesses.

Launching into a Campaign

Before your charity launches into a capital campaign, you and your board should ask the following questions:

Do you really need a campaign? What are you going to use the contributed money for? Do you think your needs will be supported by a broad base of your constituents? Can you conduct your own campaign? Many charities decide to launch into a capital campaign using staff. I can't recommend this procedure, although I have seen it work once or twice, but I have seen it fail many more times. Having outside counsel creates a sense of urgency and a timetable that must be adhered to.

When will you be ready? It is not unusual for the charity that launches into a campaign to fail because of poor timing. It

173

could be that the leaders you want to involve are already committed to one or more competing campaigns. If you elect to launch a campaign for a new gymnasium at the same time that your basketball coach has been sanctioned for improper recruiting violations, a campaign is not be a good idea.

What should the feasibility study tell you? You will never be able to predict exactly what the study will show, although you should be able to predict many of the findings in advance. The study will often confirm many of your suspicions.

To Ensure a Successful Campaign

You and your board should thoroughly examine the consultant whom you authorize to conduct the study and the campaign. If you are in the Deep South and your consultant is a fast-talking Yankee, he or she may adversely affect the information gathered. The opposite can also be true. If a slow-talking Southerner with a deep drawl interviews in the North, he, too, is likely to affect the information adversely. Talk to other charities for which the consultant has conducted campaigns. Ask how the volunteers liked the person. Did the consultant follow up with the volunteer leaders? One of the greatest things previous clients can say about the person who conducted their campaign is, "*He or she stayed on top of the volunteer workers, making sure they completed their assignments.*"

It is a good idea to design a written document outlining clearly defined responsibilities for the consultant. The executive director needs to be informed but needs to get out of the way so that the consultant can do his or her job effectively. If the executive director has confidence in the consultant, the director can become the consultant's best asset. Unfortunately, the opposite can also happen.

For best results, it is helpful if the consultant and the executive director make a commitment to work together. The executive director should facilitate whenever and wherever possible, but the consultant should have full decision-making responsibility for the campaign.

174

Capital Campaigning

A Feasibility Study

A feasibility study is an objective survey of an organization's fund-raising potential that also measures the strength of its case and the availability of its leaders, workers, and prospective donors.

The study is followed by a written report that includes the study findings, recommendations, and (when the goal is feasible) a campaign plan, timetable, and budget.

Objectives of the Feasibility Study

The objectives of the feasibility study include identification of potential leadership, the approximate amount of funds that it is thought can be raised, strengths and weaknesses of the client's organization, and correctly determined timing.

A study should include 80 to 100 interviews with people who are leaders in the community. This number of interviews is considerably more than most study consultants want to conduct. However, in every study that I conducted, only once did I interview fewer than 100. On that occasion, I interviewed 99 people.

Confidentiality

The consultant (sometimes called a study director) is ethically bound to **confidentiality**. Whatever is learned in the study that pertains to an individual is strictly confidential. No self-respecting consultant will turn over this information to a client. By the same token, the consultant is just as ethically bound to find a way to convey the information in a format that is confidential but that allows the client to decide whether or not to conduct a capital campaign. This is accomplished by a written *Report and Recommendation.*

The consultant provides one or more copies of the written report concerning his or her interpretation of the answers to the questions asked the interviewees. Usually this R&R (Report and Recommendation) lists each question and a composite of the answers. Often, several of the more important answers are listed verbatim.

Example: Have you or any member of your family ever attended the university?

Fund Raising 101

* Yes, I am a graduate and so are both of my children.
* Yes, my daughter attends the university. Good school.
* No, but I have thought many times what a good job they do with their graduates.
* No, but they produce well-rounded graduates.
* No, but they are a good corporate citizen in the community.

Get the idea? You can tell by the tone of the answers that nearly everyone you talk to in the community feels that the university is an asset to the community.

Example: Have you or any member of your family ever attended the university?
* Yes, I'm a graduate, but I'm glad I'm not there now. This president is a kook.
* Yes, my daughter attends the university. She says that the politics at the school are tearing it apart.
* No, but I have thought many times how lucky I am.

Again, get the idea? A capital campaign in this atmosphere would be a dismal failure. A feasibility study might do this university a world of good. If the president read a report like the one that would come from a study of his school, it would confirm what he has been afraid to learn. I am aware of institutions that got their act together after they saw themselves in black and white. I have also seen the president pack his bags.

Procedures in a Feasibility Study

First, the need has to be established and written down in the form of a compelling case statement. Study consultants are usually capable of doing this within a few hours. Generally, your organization will need to provide the study consultant with a chronological history of your organization, as well as how you want to use the money.

Capital Campaigning

Also at this time, a "trial" goal must be agreed on. The study will indicate how feasible this "trial" goal will be to obtain.

Second, the study consultant asks everyone who that has knowledge of people in the community to make a list of persons who they believe to be wealthy enough to contribute $10,000 or more to the charity. If a dozen or so people participate in this exercise, the prospects who are mentioned several times are likely to wind up on the list of people to be interviewed. The consultant discusses this list with the help of the executive director and prioritizes 150 to 250 people to be interviewed.

Third, a letter of introduction is written by a very important person, requesting that the addressee grant an interview to the consultant and indicating that someone will be calling soon to make an appointment for that interview.

A secretary who is knowledgeable about the geography of the community makes the appointments. Allowing for travel time, most directors like to have forty-five minutes to one hour per interview. The interview actually takes about thirty to forty minutes, but there is often an opportunity to gain additional valuable information, so you must allow time to do that.

Fourth, in the interview, an experienced study consultant asks the questions and probes for factual answers. If properly skilled, the study consultant can not only gain information that would never usually be told to an insider but can often read body or facial language that may differ from what is being said. This is one of the primary reasons for having outside counsel conduct these interviews.

Once, I had an interviewee indicate that he would not contribute anything to the campaign that I was studying. He turned out to be my first $1 million contributor! The campaign was for the private school that I mentioned in an earlier chapter. During our conversation following the interview, he discussed how important this school was to the community. Without it, many of the northern companies that were considering relocating to his southern city would not do so. Guess what? He was in real estate, and he needed the school as much or more than anyone in the community.

Fund Raising 101

The fifth and final part of the feasibility study is the report. Names of interviewees are never used. The question is listed, and all pertinent answers are listed under the question. The factors that you should be interested in are:
* Financial support available.
* Identification of existing problems.
* Identification of individuals willing to make calls and provide leadership.
* Determining if cultivation is needed.
* Identification of new prospects.
* Timing considerations.

The following additional benefits usually come from a feasibility study:
* A written report outlining your degree of preparedness to achieve a specific goal.
* An objective assessment of opinions about your institution.
* A set of recommendations outlining steps and fund-raising options.
* A written fund-raising plan.
* A third-party insight into your current donor base.
* A list of possible new donors.
* Cultivation of possible donors and campaign leaders.
* A written case statement for support.

You now have a general picture of phase 1, the feasibility study. Phase two is the organization of the campaign. We begin with inspiration.

Inspiration

A positive attitude is essential to the campaign. I was providing consultation for a state university in Kansas, in a town of about 12,000, plus the students, when their one major industry announced it was closing. I had just begun the planning and recruiting in the campaign when I received the shocking news. This

178

industry was the number one employer in the community, and this company manufactured hospital supplies. Not only was this company the number one employer, they employed more people than county government and the college put together. A meeting of the campaign's volunteer leadership was called. They discussed the possibility of ending the campaign. After all, 20 percent of the eligible donors would soon be unemployed.

After much discussion, I was beginning to see the problem. Selfishly, I was thinking that I had never had a failed campaign and didn't want this one to be my first. Just as I was about to throw in the towel, I heard myself saying, *"Wait a minute! You men and women are the leaders in this community. If you quit, what do you think the rest of the community will do? People will begin selling their houses and packing their belongings, and they will move away from this town that you all love so dearly."* Thank the Man Upstairs for inspiration. It could have been devastating for the community if we had decided to end the campaign even before it began.

At the end of the contract period, we had only $1 1/4 million. The university did hit its $2 million goal about a year later. Anyone in that town will tell you that campaign did more than provide the money to renovate a wonderful performing arts auditorium for the university. It helped to keep the pioneer spirit alive.

Planning Your Capital Campaign

Your capital campaign must be well documented. The campaign director must have numbers that validate the need. For instance, I was conducting a campaign for a hospital that needed more patient rooms. Patients were sleeping in patient beds located in the halls of the hospital. We counted the patients in the halls for ten days and discovered that nine patients per week-night slept on beds in the hall. With these facts, the need for patients' rooms was not hard to sell.

Fund Raising 101

Next, communicate these facts in a strong and compelling case statement. It is not compelling simply to state that nine people each night must sleep in the hallways of the hospital. It is far more compelling to write, "*Because of the shortage of patient rooms in our hospital, patients suffering from all kinds of sicknesses must be subjected to the noise and other indignities of sleeping in the hallway.*"

Solving the Problem

The public will not support a fund-raising effort that is obviously not going to solve the problem. If you need $5 million to build a new wing onto your hospital and you are conducting a campaign for $1 million, your public will very quickly point this fact out to you.

Be sure that you are addressing the correct problem and that a successful campaign will be adequate to fund the solution.

Selecting Leadership

As your consultant (who at this point is often referred to as the campaign director or resident consultant) plans for your campaign, he or she will be identifying the people who should hold the key leadership roles: the campaign chairman and the development chairman. These two positions are the keys to your campaign's success. A mistake here is like a circus trapeze artist failing to use a safety net. To lessen the chance for error, I have always tried to recruit co-chairpersons for these two positions.

Other tasks to be accomplished during the planning phase include the following:

1. Provide job descriptions for all the leadership roles in the campaign. Recruit sufficient number of volunteers to fill all the leadership roles as well as the solicitation roles.

2. Use careful thought in selecting the suspects (people who might become prospects) and prospects to be called upon.

3. Be sure you have adequate staff support to deal with the work load.

180

4.   Determine that the budget is adequate to carry the campaign to completion.
5.   Carry out all the recommendations of the feasibility study. (Naturally, if your organization has some history with past capital campaigns, you will have made that information available to your campaign director, who will have taken these data into consideration.)
6.   Include in the planning of the campaign the information gathered during the study concerning the community environment (for example, information about the United Way campaign and other meaningful data).

A Basic Premise

Many professional fund raisers feel that a capital campaign should be conducted periodically, every five to seven years. If you hang around fund raising for a while, you will hear the phrase, "Use them or lose them." The theory is that capital money can be raised as long as there is a sufficient case.

I wholeheartedly agree with the theory. Every time that I have conducted a capital campaign when an existing annual campaign was going on, the annual campaign suffered a loss of approximately 20 percent. However, the capital campaign raised the level of giving among the current contributors. Therefore, the annual campaign increased in subsequent years. The clients were pleased because of the increase in the annual campaign, plus the funds raised by the capital campaign made them come out far ahead.

In fact, most professional fund raisers feel that the best capital campaigns are done by and for institutions with established annual programs and that the least effective (or more difficult) campaigns occurred where there was no ongoing development activity.

The Case for Support

We examined the case statement and its significance earlier in this book. Another important use of the case statement is to document a need that your institution has. The case should also point out how your institution intends to deal with the problem.

If written properly, the case statement establishes the worthiness of the institution. It documents the sound planning that has gone into your organization's long-range plan, as well as how this project fits.

Accompanying the case statement is also all pertinent financial data and lists of the boards. And it is always helpful to have newspaper articles and letters of endorsement by experts in related fields.

Your case statement becomes the basis for subsequent printed materials, brochures, and proposals—everything that is said or written about the program.

What You Need to Be Successful

For your capital campaign to be successful you need the following:

1. You need to identify your institution's constituency. The constituency can be those people your organization serves. It can also be businesses that benefit because your organization is in the community. It can be the beneficiaries of some type of cultural activity that your organization provides to the community. Your constituency is anyone whom you serve or who may benefit by your institution's existence.

2. You need to have a thorough understanding of the problem and how your proposed plan will be a good solution. To have a thorough understanding, your constituency must be provided with adequate education. The education begins with the feasibility study and continues with correspondence from the leadership, followed by a kick-off meeting, a campaign brochure, educational meetings, and finally a personal solicitation.

3. You need to have a constituency that is receptive to your organization's solution and that agrees it deserves a high

priority. If the people who are called on do not place a very high priority on your campaign, they will not support it at the financial level that you need if you are to have a winning campaign.

4.   You will need to accept capital campaign standards of giving. Capital campaigns do not resemble any other type of fund-raising campaigns. The pool of prospects can consist of from 100 to 500 prospects who must be visited. About 60 to 80 percent of the campaign goal usually comes from around 100 of these prospects. Neither the dollar goal nor the size of the community has much effect on the number of prospects in the pool.

Figure 25 is a gift chart for a $5 million campaign in Anytown, USA.

Figure 25

Size of Gifts Needed for a $5 Million Goal

1	Gift	@	$ 1,000,000	$1,000,000
1	Gift	@	750,000	1,750,000
2	Gifts	@	500,000	2,750,000
3	Gifts	@	250,000	3,500,000
5	Gifts	@	100,000	4,000,000
5	Gifts	@	50,000	4,250,000
8	Gifts	@	25,000	4,450,000
10	Gifts	@	15,000	4,600,000
15	Gifts	@	10,000	4,750,000
20	Gifts	@	5,000	4,850,000
12	Gifts	@	2,500	4,880,000
50	Gifts	@	1,000	4,930,000
Many Gifts Under			1,000	$5,000,000

Note that the top twelve gifts equal 80 percent of the $5 million goal.

---

5.   You need the most powerful and influential leaders in your
      community. You want as leaders the individuals to whom no
      one in the community wants to say "no". These leaders need
      to be seen in the community as natural leaders whom others
      want to follow. It is extremely
      helpful, but not necessary, if they also are capable of and
      willing to make one of the lead gifts.

6.   You need to be willing to follow a plan of action that has
      been developed by an experienced capital fund raiser. One
      of the truest signs of leadership is knowing when to follow
      expert advice. However, every natural leader sometimes has
      difficulty doing this. If your leadership begins altering the
      capital campaign plan, you are doomed. All capital campaign
      companies and experienced consultants use the same basic
      principles in conducting capital campaigns. Why do they do
      so? Because the fund-raising principles used today work as
      well as they did when they were introduced in the early
      1900s.

7.   You need to be alert to the timing factor. It would be
      disastrous for you if you kicked off your campaign three
      weeks after two other organizations kicked off theirs,
      especially if they are more popular in the community than
      your organization is. You could wind up with no leadership
      or financial support.

8.   You need to have sufficient staff to support your volunteer
      activities. If you do not have the staff to arrange for the
      printing, plan the meetings, conduct the training, and so forth,
      you will have difficulty keeping your project on track.

9.   You need adequate financial support to launch a campaign.
      Although capital campaigns have the reputation   o f
      being the least expensive form of fund raising, they are not
      inexpensive. A one-year campaign costs from $120,000 to
      $240,000 in consulting fees, plus $60,000 to $100,000 for
      expenses. This is a lot of money, and it sounds like even
      more to a struggling not-for-profit organization. Yet, an

expense of $250,000 for a $5 million capital campaign is only 5 percent. Money at 5 percent is a better bargain than you will find most anywhere else. And you do not have to pay it back.

Setting Goals and Objectives

If you are to set effective goals, you need to know your charity's history in its previous capital campaigns. You also need the information that a feasibility study will have provided. It is also helpful to know how well neighboring and local peer institutions have done with their campaigns.

It is my feeling that in the past five to ten years, charities have gone from reasonable goals in campaigns to unreasonable goals. I am sure that it has a lot to do with pride, but I think the goals that many charities are using today are going to cause the public to lose patience with us. At a recent conference, I overheard someone saying that Harvard will soon be announcing a $1 billion goal. That's right -- One Billion Dollars!

It seems only yesterday that Stanford University was announcing a $100 million goal. I don't believe these capital campaign goals are as realistic as they once were. They seem to me to be hype or ego. If So-And-So University can raise $50 million, we can raise twice that amount. I'm running into clients that needed $6 to $10 million and had a realistic chance of raising that but were promised by a consultant that they could raise $50,000. Not all, but some of the consultants are suggesting that clients count annual campaign money, endowment campaign money, and anything else in with the capital campaign goal. I have trouble with the ethics of this type of campaigning.

Let's discuss the factors that you should consider when setting a goal for your campaign. Begin by reviewing the history of your organization. If it has had campaigns before, what were their goals? What did the feasibility study tell you? Although the consultant will keep confidential the study information as it applies to certain individuals, he or she will tell you what has been learned about the potential top ten gifts. A few years ago, I was asked to visit a college campus in a neighboring state that had a $75 million capital campaign goal. After eighteen months, the only money raised came from planned giving and the annual campaign. The company that was conducting the campaign had produced the best-looking brochures that I have even laid my eyes on, but they had not produced any financial support for their client.

The school I am referring to had been seduced into believing that it could solicit the same kind of financial support that a Stanford or Harvard could. They had only 1,300 students, were located in a town of fewer than 3,000 people, and were within 100 miles of the state university and a dozen other schools. The constituency of a small-town college is its alumni, parents, and local businesses. This school has ceased trying to be a quality small school and wants to be the equal of Harvard, Yale, and Princeton. The reality is that they will never be the equal of those great institutions. Their alumni have been worn out by phon-a-thons, direct mail, personal visits, and anything else that can be done by the school to build support.

I am not denigrating the school's effort. I am saying only that it has ceased being a good corporate citizen and may have become a corporate nuisance. It would have been well advised to have a $5 to $10 million campaign, or whatever the feasibility study recommended. The consulting company's fee for services was $19,000 a month for three years. The college finally bailed out after 20 months when there had not yet been a nickel raised.

I mention this story because you need to know that if a consultant's promised result sounds too good to be true, it probably is.

Back to your organization. If there has never been a campaign larger than $3 million, you are taking a big risk to jump out with a $30 million campaign. You had better have the *mother* of all compelling cases.

Evaluation (Also Known as Rating)
Evaluation is the process of identifying sources of large gifts

186

and the potential for a thoughtful and proportionate gift. Evaluation should answer the question, *"How much might this prospect give if interested and asked by the right person?"*

Evaluation is a painstaking process that must include key volunteer leaders who are involved, informed, and knowledgeable about potential donors. Evaluation must be in relation to the required standards of giving—the top gift, and the top ten, and the top 100. Amounts must be both realistic and challenging.

A most important part of goal setting is evaluating your prospects. Assuming you have already identified approximately 500 prospects, you must now evaluate them. Select about five individuals from your community to do the evaluating. These people should be knowledgeable about the personal finances on members of the community, and they should be promised that their names will be kept in strictest confidence.

At a meeting, provide each evaluator with an alphabetic list of the 500 prospects. Some consultants like to use 3-by-5-inch cards with the names of each prospect on a separate card. They call the names out one at a time, and the evaluators suggest an amount to ask from the prospect. No matter which method you use, all prospects must be carefully considered for their ability to give. Of course, the evaluations are only estimates, but they will be fairly accurate if the evaluators are truly familiar with your town's folks.

After all 500 prospects have been evaluated, the amounts estimated should be at least three times larger than the campaign goal. The reason for this is that a capital campaign usually only raises about one third of the total amount of the evaluations. Therefore, if your goal is $5 million and your evaluations equal $15 million, you have a good chance of succeeding.

I realize that you will find this process difficult to go along with, especially if this is the first time you have ever heard of it. However, smarter people than I will tell you that it has to be this way.

Fund Raising 101

Sources of Support

Campaigns are usually divided into two broad divisions: the internal and the external divisions. The internal division, sometimes referred to as the family division, is further divided into employees, boards, auxiliary (if applicable), doctors for a hospital, teachers for a college, and so forth. The external division is further divided into several groups that may include prospects of very large potential, medium potential, and a more modest potential. The prospects in a division are usually determined by size, not business types. In other words, you might find small and large businesses, individuals, and maybe even foundations in the divisions comprising $1,000 prospects. By the same token, you might find a similar mix in the division containing prospects with a potential of $25,000.

For internal support, you should be able to count on the board of your institution for sacrificial support. After all, if the board is not going to give at a level that is considered generous, why should anyone else? Do not overlook the employees. They too, should be willing to give at a level that would be considered generous for their income. Other groups to be considered include members of your organization or the auxiliary.

The names of the various groups is not all that critical. You might name the external divisions Pattern, Advance, Special, and Foundations, or any other names that you wish.

The Campaign Plan

The campaign plan outlines all activities and indicates completion dates. It fixes responsibility and job descriptions of the leadership, volunteers, board, and staff. It also includes outlines of the organizational requirements, timetables, deadlines, job descriptions, prospect review procedures, publicity plan, record keeping and mechanical aspects, and campaign policies. All these are provided by the campaign consultant, but they must be approved by the campaign steering committee. The steering committee should be made up of the campaign chairman, development chairman, and the chairmen from the other division leaders.

Capital Campaigning

The day-to-day responsibility for managing the campaign belongs to the consultant.

To be successful in a capital campaign, it is necessary to have a deep commitment from a nucleus of top-level leadership. The authority and control for the campaign should be placed in the hands of the campaign consultant, who is responsible for the flow of information to and through the organization, the board, and staff. The consultant must be fully informed of the other areas of campaigning that might be going on, such as the annual campaign, planned giving, special events, and the like. The consultant must have the full and complete cooperation of the charity's staff, administration, business office, computer, PR and marketing, maintenance, housekeeping, and food service, as well as access to records of donors, past and present board members, corporations, foundations, friends, and so on.

Selecting the Leadership

During the feasibility study, interviewees are asked to name an individual or individuals who they feel are best suited to provide leadership in the campaign that has been described to them. One, two, or three people usually will be identified repeatedly as the most qualified to lead because they are closely identified with the charity or they are well known for providing leadership for these types of campaigns.

As we come to the end of this chapter, let us review the three major phases of a capital campaign:
- The feasibility study.
- The planning--length, timing, volunteer and staff support, the case for support.
- The implementation--identifying prospects, targeting gifts, solicitation, and monitoring results.

If you have a competent campaign consultant, you will have a successful and enjoyable campaign.

Fund Raising 101

Chapter Sixteen

Grant Writing

Grants are described as the voluntary transfer of resources to private nonprofit organizations or individuals by governments, private foundations, and corporations.

Personally, I regard grant writing as the least understood, and yet it is among the most pursued avenues of fund gathering today. During the late 1960s and most of the 1970s, grants were readily available, especially from government sources. This abundant availability created a myth that still prevails: that grants are available simply for the asking. This misconception would not be a problem except that the government "well" began drying up to the point that unless you were pursuing grants for something to do with AIDS, you would not have much chance of getting one. With few exceptions, only those people who are persistent and creative and who have the time to pursue grants will find them today. Even private foundations that exist for the sole purpose of providing grants to 501(c)(3) organizations require more creativity and accountability than in years past.

Many newcomers to our profession think of grants as just another source of funds. However, the foundations making the grants view granting as a means of encouraging social change and of testing high-risk ideas. The grantors appear to prefer to support new programs. Therefore, those charities that have effective grant programs strive to tailor a proposal that will enhance and expand an existing program. They apply new and innovative methods of delivering their service and at the same time try meet the grantors' criteria for new, innovative, or experimental programs. Therefore, if you are to tackle grantsmanship as part of your fund-raising arsenal, you may need to alter your perception of grant writing.

I am not trying to discourage you from writing proposals for grants. On the contrary, I encourage you to learn as much as you can about how the process works and to take the plunge. My hope is to make you understand that if you have limited resources and must feed a hungry operating budget, grantsmanship will not easily fill that need.

How to Go About Applying for a Grant

Let's start with a few tips. If you and your charity are going to launch into a grant process, here are a few things you should know:

1. Begin by identifying the proposal deadline for the grant for which you wish to apply. By beginning preparations early, you will have plenty of time to prepare your applications properly. The charities that are successful at locating grants and securing them are those that start early.
2. Do not try to get too fancy with your grant applications. Managers of the federal grant programs state that the application process is really very simple. Read the application instructions thoroughly, and follow them carefully. If you have any questions, call the number they provide.
3. Clearly state the purpose of your request early in the proposal. Include a compelling statement about who will be served and how. Include adequate documentation and explain how your project is unique.
4. Develop a good report and evaluation system and keep the grantor informed of the progress that takes place.

If you work in a large agency with plenty of employees, you can assign grant writing responsibility to one or more people, and they can begin the learning process. However, this book is intended for those individuals who are new to the process or who have had some experience as fund raisers. Well, then, how can the beginning fund raiser participate?

Volunteers! With your guidance, volunteers can learn the process of grant writing and can accomplish the job handily. In fact, if you are looking for creativity in your applications for grants, volunteer-driven grant writing is a good start.

The process of seeking support from granting sources is primarily one of thoughtful and careful planning, involving a process of research, cultivation, proposal writing, and sometimes making oral presentations. It has been said that grant writing is 10 percent inspiration and 90 percent perspiration.

In you elect to involve a volunteer, you will be looking for the type of person who enjoys the solitude of reading, working crossword puzzles—a retired librarian, lawyer, proofreader, anyone who has above average reading, writing, and research skills. Once you have located one or more of this type of volunteer, you are ready to begin.

Where to Start

Start with organization and planning. First, identify the grantors who have interests that are similar to those of your charity. This is where research becomes pertinent. Determine the following:

* If your philosophies are similar.
* If you can meet the restrictions that they require.
* If your interests are compatible.
* If you can meet their deadlines.
* If they will fund a grant of the size you are requesting.

There are two broad categories of grantors: government agencies and private foundations. The government tends to provide its grants to whatever is politically popular—education for the children of migrant workers, homeless shelters, AIDS, and so forth.

193

Government grants require elaborate reporting mechanisms that often require additional staff or volunteer time. For these reasons, only larger organizations tend to pursue government grants.

More grant variety is in the private foundations, and they are less strict in reporting requirements. However, successful grantsmanship requires an understanding of the many types and sources of available support and the regulations that determine the giving policies of each source. For these reasons, we address only private foundations in this chapter.

Private foundations fall into one of four categories:
* Company-sponsored
* Independent
* Community
* Operating

Company-sponsored foundations receive their financial support from a *for-profit* corporation. Their purpose is to make grants to a wide range of charities. They tend to support those charities that provide an outcome in which they have a particular interest. For example, if the foundation is funded by a chemical company, it makes sense for them to support a college with an excellent chemical engineering school.

Independent foundations are usually funded by one person or a family. They are sometimes referred to as *special purpose*, *general purpose*, or *family* foundations. The major purpose of the independent foundation is to make grants, usually covering a wide range of interests. However, many independent foundations have a very narrow scope. A foundation in Mississippi was established as a private foundation for the express purpose of providing college educations for the high school graduates of only one county in the state. Every high school graduate who is a resident of that county can have a free college education if they want it and can qualify academically.

194

Grant Writing

Community foundations have a general charitable purpose. They resemble private foundations except that their assets come from the contributions of many people rather than from only one person or one family. In addition, community foundations are usually classified under the United States tax law as public charities, and because of this they are subject to different rules and regulations than are private foundations.

Operating foundations usually control large endowments or a fund that has only one main purpose such as conducting research or maybe to fund a social program.

Definition of a Public Charity

A public charity is a 501(c)(3) organization that is not a private foundation, either because it is "publicly supported" (that is, **it normally derives at least one-third of its support from gifts and other qualified sources**) or it functions as a "supporting organization" to other public charities. Some public charities engage in grant-making activities, but most engage in direct service activities. Public charities are eligible for maximum tax-deductible contributions from the public and are not subject to the same rules and restrictions as private foundations. They are also referred to as "public foundations." The hospital foundation that employs me fits this description.

Steps in the Grant Application Process

You now know what grantsmanship is, what foundations are, and what a charity is. It is time to learn the steps in the grant application process. There are **Nine**

Logical Steps:
1. Research and prepare for the visit.
2. Identify and know as much as possible about your prospect.
3. Make an appointment.

4. **Visit your prospect.**
5. **Share your reason for being there.**
6. **Ask for the investment.**
7. **Know how to handle objections.**
8. **Be persistent and follow up.**
9. **Write a thank-you note.**

To organize and prepare a grant application properly, you will spend about 60 percent of your time doing the research and about 40 percent writing the proposals.

If you are to be successful in grantsmanship, you must acquire some resource books such as *The Foundation Directory*. You can get more information about *The Foundation Directory* by calling 1-800-424-9836. The directory contains most of the foundations located in the United States. They are listed alphabetically with addresses, phone numbers, history, the types of programs they support, officers, and how to communicate with them.

Recently, I read that *The Foundation Directory* has added more than 1,000 new foundations since their last issue. This should give you a feel as to why there is a great deal of research necessary. Comb through the book and find only those grantors that support the program you are establishing. Gather as much specific information on each prospective grantor as you can. It could turn out that one of your volunteers knows one of the members of a grantor's board. It could be that someone on the grantor's board came from your community. You can see how that could be helpful to you.

Eliminate all the grantors that do not fund your mission. Once you have identified the prospects that have interests that match your needs, you are ready to move on to the next step: evaluating.

At this point, I am going to add corporations in with the foundations. A large corporation located in or near your community can be the source of a terrific grant, so do not overlook them. Take a look at their current profit-and-loss statement, which could tell you whether they could help you if you called on them. Determine the relevance of the business to your organization and the community.

196

Grant Writing

What products do they produce? It would not do for MADD, Mothers Against Drunk Driving, to apply for a grant from a liquor company. If you can, determine who controls the giving. You might hurt your chances for a grant if you write the president, who turns out to be a figurehead, when the executive vice president is really the person in charge.

For foundation grantors, look at their assets, annual distribution, and the size of grants that they fund. If you are seeking a grant of $100,000 and the foundation you are about to write a proposal to never funds anything larger than $25,000, you have a problem. Of course, the problem can be solved if you write the grant in such a way as to meet their requirements. All pertinent information can be found in *The Foundation Directory*.

Determine in advance if there are likely to be strings on the grant once you have it. For example, a hospital needs a new cancer wing, but a donor gives $10 million for a new physical fitness center. If you are the director of fund raising for your hospital, what do you do? Do you take the gift? Do you not take the gift? Obviously, the hospital administrator and the board are the ones to make this decision. But it could create a dilemma.

Cultivation is the next step to consider. You want the grantor to know as much about your institution as possible. Just recently, I heard of a woman who wanted to get the attention of a major grant-making foundation. She sent them special delivery letters every day for a week. The next week she called every day. The third week she went back to special delivery letters. On the third day of the third week they called her. By the way, these letters were not nuisance letters. They contained very carefully thought out communications.

Once you have identified a prospect foundation, call or write to them for information about how to submit a grant request. They are usually gracious and helpful. Remember, their assets are exempt from taxes; therefore, their assets are public domain in a way. The assets are there for a stated purpose, and if they aren't used accordingly, the foundation will have to answer to the IRS.

In the case of a nearby corporation, you can visit, ask questions, and get to know the principals involved. Invite them to visit your office. Let them see your plans. Get input from them. You can see how this type of hands-on approach may bring the funding source into contact with the program.

After you have conducted all the research and provided opportunity for involvement (if possible), it is time to build your proposal, including your case. Elsewhere in this book I have said that a case must be compelling. If you can't make your case compelling, you may lose out to another charity that can.

What a Grant Proposal Should Look Like

Proposals are usually written for one of three grantor audiences: private foundations, government agencies, or corporations. A proposal, not including the back-up material, should not exceed ten pages for foundations and government and five pages for corporations. Back-up materials should not exceed another ten pages for foundations and government agencies and five pages for corporations.

Your proposal can be assembled in many ways. One way includes the following:

- A title page.
- Contents page.
- Project description (for what and how the money will be spent).
- Methods by which the donor will receive visibility.
- Statement of the case.
- Statement of organizational stability (as an organization, how will you institute this project?).
- Statement of staff proficiency (is staff adequate?).
- Method by which you plan to communicate progress (how will the donor know about the progress being made?).
- A brief history of your institution.
- A realistic budget.

Grant Writing

Back-up materials:
- 501(c)(3) federal tax exemption.
- Volunteer leadership (list officers and board with full names, companies, and mailing addresses).
- A list of any experts who will be associated with the grant (one-page résumés are in order).
- An outline of previous successes with other grants (newspaper and magazine articles are helpful). (If you don't have previous grants, list a few major corporate gifts.)
- Letters from individuals who have benefitted by previous grants.

Make an Appointment

If you want to visit a local corporation in behalf of your charity, have the person who is most likely to be able to get an appointment for you to call for the appointment. It can be a staffer. It can be a volunteer. It makes little difference who makes the appointment as long as it's done. You don't want to lose out at this stage.

Asking for the Investment

Again, the right volunteers (often the most influential) should participate in the presentation.

At this point, I should mention that there is a raging debate going on about who should make the presentation. Some say the volunteers, others say the staff. I feel that the individual who has the most influence and the ability to present the proposal in a logical format is the one who should make the presentation. The exception would be when it makes no difference to the prospect who makes the proposal; he has already decided that he is going to give support only to his golfing partner. Although research will help you in most situations, it may not have helped you in this scenario.

It would be a million-to-one shot for me to be in a position to make a presentation without the accompaniment of a volunteer or volunteers.

Fund Raising 101

Any salesman will tell you that sooner or later you are going to have to ask for the order. And we have a better chance of success if the person asking for the order is a very influential person. Most grant-seekers now refer to the gift as an investment, which makes a lot of sense because we are talking about the improvement of the community, the lives of its residents, or something of that nature.

If you prepare a written proposal for a nearby foundation and it will be delivered by mail, consider the proper signature on the proposal. Add the right person to the right time and you have a powerful duo. But think how catastrophic it would be if on the day you were calling on a foundation in person, they were having a retirement party for their president. Timing is important. Another reason to have an appointment.

Follow Up

If you have the opportunity to make a personal call, attempt to have your thank-you letters in the mail within twenty-four hours. The same is true if you receive a *yes* or a *no* through the mail. If you receive a *no*, spend some time trying to determine the reason you were turned down. This type of information can be helpful to you in the future when you prepare other grant requests.

If you receive support of a grant request, you are now obligated to provide the information and updates that you outlined in your grant proposal. If you do not honor this obligation, you will never again be able to gain support from this grantor. It's a good idea to include progress reports and information about any new developments.

An annual report telling about progress being made is generally all that is required by private foundations.

Recognition

It is important that you know the type of recognition that your grantor would find most appropriate. For example, they could be very upset if you identified them in the newspaper when they were trying to keep everyone from knowing that they have money for grants. Or if they are struggling with employees over wages, you could hurt the negotiations if word of your grant got out. You can learn how to respond by simply asking how best you can recognize their gift. Many corporations want their employees to know that they support local charities, such as the United Way, arts, hospitals, colleges, and so on.

General Information

Sometimes general information about your charity is helpful—or example, the number of their employees who use your institution, the number of students who graduated with a degree in engineering, the number of employees who visit your art shows, and the like.

Describe the economic effect that your project will have on the community. Most chambers of commerce demonstrate the impact of a new business by telling the prospect that for every dollar spent in the community, an additional $7 will be generated throughout the economy.

There is one thing of which you can be certain: when it comes to government grants, what is available today will soon not be available. To secure government grants, you have to get on top of information dealing with them and stay there.

Information about Corporations and Why They Give

The average CEO of a corporation decides where to place the company's contributions. However, most CEOs agree that their board of directors have a tremendous influence on the company's giving. Corporations give for a number of reasons. The following are some of the most important:

* To improve the quality of life in communities where they operate and where their employees live.
* For tax benefits.
* Their generosity helps to build a positive public image.
* To support programs that enhance their business or skills.
* Sometimes they are returning a favor.

Fund Raising 101

* Often serves to improve relations with employees.
* Peer pressure by other corporations.
* It is felt that giving will stimulate sales.
* Because of the CEO and/or the board members who want to give.
* As a reward to employees.
* Matching the gifts of employees.

Grants to various types of charities break down to the following approximations:

*	Arts & Culture	14.0%
*	Education	22.2%
*	Environment & Animals	4.9%
*	Health	17.3%
*	Human Services	15.2%
*	International Affairs	3.9%
*	Public and Social Benefit	10.0%
*	Science & Social Science	11.0%
*	Religion	1.4%
*	All Others	0.1%

All right, you should be ready to begin the recruiting and training of your volunteers. And we hope that in a very short time you will be sending out your first grant requests.

Part Three

Chapter Seventeen

Proposal Writing

This chapter answers the following questions:
1. What is a proposal?
2. What is a proposal used for?
3. How is a proposal organized?

What Is a Proposal?

A proposal is a written document used to ask for and win the financial support of a business, corporation, foundation, or individual.

What Is a Proposal Used For?

A proposal is used as a method of putting your case (your reason for needing money) in front of a prospect in such a way as to ask for support and provide the answers to questions the prospect is likely to ask.

How Is a Proposal Organized?

The remainder of this chapter addresses the organization of a proposal.

Not all proposals need to look like the samples used as an example in this chapter. The sample proposal has more detail than you would normally need. However, this particular proposal was presented to more than 100 prospects, and seventy-one contributed to the campaign.

Fund Raising

Proposal Outline
Written proposals should be at least five, but not more than ten, pages with five to ten pages of back-up materials.
1.   The title page should include: (See Figure 26.)
  a.   Project Name.
  b.   No more than a five- or six-line description of the project.

Example: The ABC Food Pantry is requesting that (name of prospect) give consideration to investing (amount) in the process of feeding over 1,500 men, women, and children monthly.

2.   The Table of Contents page. (See Figure 27.)
3.   Project description (one or two pages on how you intend to spend the prospect's money and who will benefit).
4.   Statement of need (the case).
5.   A paragraph or two on the stability of the organization (or you can use a financial statement).
6.   If appropriate, include a paragraph or two on how the project will be staffed.
7.   A paragraph or two on how you intend to measure results and how you intend to communicate progress to the donor.
8.   Statement of how the donor will receive recognition or visibility.
9.   A brief history of your institution (no more than one page).
10.   A realistic budget.

Back-Up Materials (Exhibits)
This section should be separated in such a way that the prospect can easily tell that it contains the exhibits.
1.   A letter certifying your 501(c)(3) federal tax exemption status.
2.   Letter of assurance from the CEO of the charity giving assurance that the money will be used as the proposal indicates.

204

3.   List of volunteer leadership (list officers and board with full names, companies, and mailing addresses).

4.   List of any experts who will be associated with the grant (one-page résumés are in order).

5.   Outline of previous successes with other grants (newspaper and magazine articles are helpful if you have not had previous grants; list of a few major corporate gifts).

6.   Letters from individuals who have benefitted by previous grants.

The Final Document

1.   Must be neat, professional, and attractive.

2.   Must have names spelled correctly, with their correct titles.

3.   Must meet submission deadline.

4.   Be sure to keep a copy.

5.   Other Uses for Proposals

    a.   As a guide to prepare other proposals.

    b.   To refer to when writing letters about the effort.

    c.   For preparing speeches.

    d.   For submitting other grants.

NOTE: This format is the same one you would use to write either grant requests or capital campaign proposals. The following is the proposal mentioned at the beginning of this chapter. The capital campaign portion was for $6 million. A bond issue took place at the same time to retire old debt and to launch a $58.2 million building project.

Your proposal should be in some sort of book format. The plastic spine works well with a heavy stock paper for a front and back.

Figure 26 is the ask page. This one is an example. I don't claim its the best I've ever seen—just that it worked in this case with many gifts.

Figure 26   Page 1 - The Ask Page

THE $6,000,000
CENTENNIAL CAMPAIGN
FOR
ABC REGIONAL MEDICAL CENTER
ANYTOWN, USA

In celebration of a century of service to (your state's) residents, the Board of Directors of ABC Regional Medical Center has outlined a comprehensive $58.2 million Master Plan which will include a $6,000,000 Centennial Campaign. The plan calls for modernizing, upgrading, and enhancing programs and services, thereby enabling the Medical Center to enter the second century in the strongest, most viable leadership position.

The leadership of the $6,000,000 Centennial Campaign requests that: *The XYZ Foundation*, its management, and Board of Directors consider support of the $6,000,000 Centennial Campaign in the amount of $100,000. The funds will be used for modernizing, upgrading, and enhancing programs and services.

Additional materials explaining and documenting the need and the expected results follow. Should anyone have additional questions or wish an on-site visit, please feel free to call (010) 004-0005.

Figure 27 is the table of contents page. Usually a colored page follows separating the rest of the book into two sections, the project information and the exhibits.

Proposal Writing

Figure 27   **Page 2**

Table of Contents

Plan of Development	Page ?
The $6.0 Million Capital Campaign	Page ?
Project Description	Page ?
History of the Charity	Page ?
The Need and the Cost	Page ?
Charity's Financial Statement	Page ?
Donor Recognition	Page ??

Exhibits

501(c)(3) letter	Page ??
Letter of Assurance	Page ??
Board of Directors	Page ??
Campaign Leadership	Page ??
Charity's Balance Sheet	Page ??

Figures 28, 29, and 30 are parts of the first half of your proposal. Numbers 1 through 6 are also suggested pieces you may wish to include.

207

Fund Raising

Figure 28   Page 5

Project Description

The most dramatic and visible element in ABC's Master Plan is the construction of a new $23.0 million, multi-story, 205,000 square-foot diagnostic/high-tech building. An additional $11.0 million has been earmarked for site work, parking, furnishings and equipment. This new structure will house essential laboratory services of the Medical Center as well as radiology, and radiation therapy departments. Several ancillary services will be relocated from existing areas in order to achieve consolidation of these services in a single building. This will provide greater access and convenience for patients, physicians, and staff.

The Master Plan also calls for a significant investment in newer, more sophisticated medical technology to help maintain ABC's competitive edge well into the 21st century. This includes items such as a gamma camera, support computer for the Nuclear Medicine Department, an additional linear accelerator for use in cancer treatment, and many other new high-tech devices.

Other major items included in the Master Plan are:
* $3.0 million to renovate and modernize existing facilities.

* $3.3 million to acquire additional property for future expansion.

* $3.5 million to establish a clinical research fund to help underwrite start-up costs, to purchase equipment, and to enhance research programs like those provided by the Midwest Heart and Vascular Institute and the Orthopedic Research Institute.

* $1.0 million to provide a patient assistance fund for financial aid to patients and their families who require care from one of ABC's Centers of Excellence. This is a high-priority item and one that is vital to the continuation of the Medical Center's commitment to its mission. ABC has never, in its 100 years of existence, turned anyone away because of an inability to pay. Each year, ABC provides millions of dollars in uncompensated care to the unemployed, uninsured, and truly needy.

208

Figure 29

Almost a century ago, five Catholic nuns from the congregation of the Sisters of the Sorrowful Mother in Rome, Italy, arrived in Anytown, (Your State), to serve as the original staff for ABC Hospital. Their stated mission was "to pray and care for the unserved who suffered." This event occurred in 1889 and represented the establishment of the first American mission for the relatively new community of Sisters founded by Mother Frances Leterit in Rome in 1883.

(Follow with important milestones, i.e. first new wing, first pediatrician, etc., etc.)

GROWING . . . BUILDING . . . REACHING OUT:

ABC has come a long way from the early days when it operated from a three-story house, having only 12 patient beds. In fact, it has grown to become one of the largest non-profit medical centers in the country, and through its expanded role as a regional referral center, teaching hospital, and clinical research center, ABC touches the lives of literally thousands of (your states) residents each year. To better reflect this expanded role, the hospital was renamed ABC Regional Medical Center in 1982.

Situated on a 40-acre campus in the heart of Anytown, the Medical Center has total assets of more than $209 million. To depict in words the size and regional importance of ABC Regional Medical Center, consider the following:

1.   There are more than 1 million square feet of floor space within the Medical Center's facilities.
2.   The Medical Center's campus is composed of the main patient care building, which houses 576 fully staffed patient beds, five intensive care units, and 20 surgical suites; several medical specialty centers; three medical office buildings; several physicians' office buildings; a parking garage; and much more.
3.   A medical staff of more than 500 admit nearly 22,000 patients yearly, of whom more than 25 percent live outside the immediate area.
4.   Outpatient treatments recorded by ABCs' various medical specialty centers number more than 100,000 annually.
5.   The average daily census of over 400 patients makes ABC one of the largest inpatient healthcare providers in (your state).
6.   More than 2,500 area residents are employed at an annual payroll in excess of $65 million, making ABC one of (your state's) top employers.
7.   An annual expenditure of more than $60 million for goods and services is required to operate the physical facilities of the Medical Center, and most of these funds flow directly or indirectly into the local economy.

While constantly striving to remain at the forefront in patient care and medical technology, ABC has recorded many notable achievements, including:

1.   Developed (your state's) prestigious burn center.
2.   Developed the first and only comprehensive epilepsy program in (your state) — a program that is one of seven serving the entire nation.
3.   Established (your state's) first freestanding dialysis center.

Figure 29   Page 8

POSITIONING ABC REGIONAL MEDICAL CENTER AS A LEADER IN
ITS SECOND CENTURY:

As large and impressive as ABC Regional Medical Center is today
in its size and range of services, its employees still remain as firmly committed
to the original healthcare mission of the Sisters of the Sorrowful Mother as were
the founding Sisters almost 100 years ago. Their primary concern always will
be for the health and well-being of each individual patient, regardless of color,
nationality, religious belief, or ability to pay.

Strategic, comprehensive planning has brought ABC Regional
Medical Center to its present stature as one of the nation's top medical centers.
Patients are referred to ABC from all across (your state), as well as from many
other states. Yet, ABC's staff knows that as demographics change and as
medical knowledge and technology continue to advance, services must be
designed to respond to these changes for the Medical Center to remain at the
forefront in patient care, medical education, and research. In the past year
alone, ABC spent more than $14.4 million on capital equipment and
improvements in keeping pace with changes in the healthcare marketplace.

Recently, to project the future needs of the Medical Center, ABC's
Board of Directors concluded a comprehensive self-study as part of the
continuing planning process. The study was necessary for two primary reasons:

1.   Concern for the continued availability and accessibility of healthcare
        for the people of (your state), especially those residing in the
        Medical Center's service area.

2.   A strong desire to maintain ABC's leadership role as a quality,
        compassionate healthcare provider.

From this study emerged a plan designed to place the Medical Center
in the best possible position to enter its second century. This plan affords the
most solid financial base possible, while equipping ABC with the most modern,
up-to-the-minute equipment and facilities.

210

Proposal Writing

Figures 33 and 34 are to go in the second half of your proposal, the exhibit section, along with numbers 7 through 12.

The following pages are where you insert:

1.   Information you have showing your organizations stability.
2.   Financial information. (See the following example.)

Example:
Financial situation — The Sisters of the Sorrowful Mother have been prudent in the management of ABC Medical Center. ABC's currents assets total $206,302,976 and its liabilities are only $20,888,673. Indeed, ABC Medical Center is positioned perfectly for launching the Centennial Campaign for the Future.

3.   A statement listing or explaining your staffing.
A paragraph on the staff wasn't necessary for this hospital proposal. In others it might be appropriate, such as a child care program in which registered child care specialist might be an advantage.

4   Measurement and reporting is covered here. Try to explain how you will measure the success of the project.
A paragraph on measurement and reporting may not be necessary for this project. We did indicate to the XYZ Foundation, in the paragraph on recognition, that we would send them an update each six months.

5.   Recognition—The support provided by The XYZ Foundation will be pooled with that of other contributors, expected to number in the area of 1,825. The campaign support is likely to come from: 100% of the 35 board members and administrators, 1,100 of the employees, 325 of the physicians,

300 of the local businesses and industry, 50 local individuals, and with your involvement, 15 foundations.

Fund Raising

a. The XYZ Foundation may select any recognition from those identified for the gift amount. Naturally, should the Foundation contribute more than you requested, they may also select from designated opportunities equal to that support. If the Foundation accepts our recommendation, a tasteful plaque will be appropriately placed for maximum visibility in the employee dinning room, and from that day forward, it will be known and identified as the ABC Foundation Dining Room.

b. Periodic updates of the construction will be forwarded to The XYZ Foundation at least twice annually and will continue for two years after the building has been in use.

c. Tours will be indefinitely available to the Foundation's Board of Directors and to anyone else for whom the Foundation requests a tour.

6. **Budget** — This is the normal place for the budget. However, we included the budget with the case statement. In this instance, we included it with the project description.

There is no hard and fast rule in building your proposal. Try to put yourself in the place of the reader. If the reader is likely to want additional information at a particular place in the proposal, then it should be there. Its place in the proposal should be identified in the Contents.

The next section is for the exhibits (back-up materials).

7. Beginning with a facsimile of an IRS 501(c)(3))

8. It's common to list board members, especially if there are outstanding members of the board. Listing board members assures the granting organization that there is local participation.

9. A financial statement is appropriate.

10. If your project involved experts, include them in this section of your proposal.

212

Proposal Writing

11. Next, list other successful grants, include newspaper articles and/or grants from other notable companies. Everyone wants to get onboard a winner.
12. Finally, letters of support from the people who are being served could be helpful.

Figure 34   Letter of Assurance

ABC REGIONAL MEDICAL CENTER
October 14, 1987

To Whom It May Concern:

As President and Chief Executive Officer of ABC Regional Medical Center, Anytown, (your state), I want to assure potential donors that all gifts made to the Centennial Campaign will be used to maximum advantage in our $58.2 million Master Plan of Development.

No funds granted to the ABC Centennial Campaign will be used for any activities prohibited by the 1969 Tax Reform Act.

Sincerely,

Sister M. Morgan
President and Chief Executive Officer

MSM/td

Fund Raising

Figure 33   A sample 501(c)(3) Letter

Department of the Treasury

Internal Revenue Service
Washington, DC 20224

September 11, 1973

ABC Foundation
929 North St. Francis
Anytown, State 14245

Gentlemen:

Based on the information you recently submitted, we have classified your organization as one that is not a private foundation as defined in section 509(a) of the Internal Revenue Code because you are an organization described in the following Code Section:

_____ Sec. 509(a)(1)

_____ Sec. 509(a)(2)

_____ Sec. 509(a)(3)

_____ Sec. 509(a)(4)

This classification is based on the assumption that your operations will continue as stated in your notification. All changes in your purposes, character, or method of operation must be reported to your District Director so he can consider their effect on your status.

Sincerely yours,

Chief, Rulings Section
Exempt Organizations Branch Office

Chapter Eighteen

The Benefits of Evaluation

Evaluation of your fund-raising practices can be one of the most valuable functions you can perform for your projects, programs, and the all-around gathering of information about your charity's effectiveness. You should have a formalized system for collecting the information needed to plan for next year and the years to come. You get that data by an effective evaluation process.

Types of Information Needed

You need basic data, such as the number of donors who participated in each project, the total dollars raised and spent, the average gift size, and the like.

Job Descriptions

You also need job descriptions. Some job descriptions are general, but others must be more specific. Those that are specific must be precise in terms and percentages of time to be spent on each project or program, the dollars to be raised, and so on.

These descriptions are reviewed annually for accuracy. You need job descriptions for each staff member as well as for the various volunteer positions. As an example, the following is a general job description for a board member.

Board Member

1. **Board members must make sure that their charity meets the needs of the people they represent and the people the charity serves.** The organization exists to serve others. The bottom line of every decision a board member makes should be, "How will this decision help us serve people better?"

2. **Board members, as a group, set policies and goals that the executive director implements.** Board members do not carry out policy. That is why the board hired an executive. The board should allow the executive to implement its decisions.

It is also important to understand that board members do not take action as individuals; they must act as a team. Board members who take board actions without the approval of the full board may seriously damage the organization.

3. **Board members must ensure that their organization has adequate finances and approve an annual budget so that money can be responsibly spent.** No board can set policy and make plans for the future without understanding and making plans for adequate financing. All board members should contribute their personal influence and resources to ensure that the organization has the proper funds to conduct policy directives.

As "trustees" of the organization's money, board members have the fiduciary responsibility of seeing that it is spent prudently. This, however, does not mean that they must approve every expenditure. It does mean that they know the money was spent effectively to deliver the kind of programs and services that they have authorized. Fiscal accountability can be achieved by having a finance committee that oversees expenditures on a monthly basis.

The Benefits of Evaluation

4.   Board members must play an active role in supporting the organization and the administrator. One of the primary responsibilities of board members is to support the executive director . . . not to give the administrator daily orders but to be supportive of the board's policies. Their role is to provide the direction in which they want the executive to take the organization. And they must also provide the executive with the necessary resources and the authority needed to get the job done.

Once the board gives their executive direction and resources, they should let the executive freely manage the organization. Expect feedback from the executive on performance of the organization, and evaluate the executive on this performance. The board members should not expect feedback from the executive concerning individual employees. They delegated management of individual employees to the executive when the executive was hired.

Board members make decisions that affect the whole organization. The executive director makes decisions that affect individuals in the organization, such as staff members.

5.   Board members, acting as a full board, select and evaluate a chief executive officer, who in turn becomes the board's manager. Board members must nurture their executive by providing adequate compensation and reasonable direction. Because the executive is the board's only employee, they should give him or her a written job description and be explicit about what they expect. They must let the executive know what the board wants, and then stand back and let the executive do it!

6.   Board members should support the executive with their consulting skills—when asked. Their personal skills are valuable to the executive director and the organization. For example, the board may include a tax attorney, and the organization may desperately need tax advice. But remember, when board members volunteer for non-board work, they do so as an individual—not as a board member. Like anyone who volunteers to work for the organization, they are under the direct control of the executive director.

Thus, a board member should not just jump in and assess the need for a new computer without the executive's approval. It's a little tricky when a board member's role changes from board member to volunteer when non-board work is involved, but the rewards are well worth it! In which area does the organization need volunteers? What skills does a board member have that might help fill this need? Talk to the executive director!

7.   **Board members, acting as a team, should make a written plan that outlines the long-term future of the organization (five to ten years).** The executive formulates and carries out the short-term plan (one year or less).

Two problems frequently occur. The first is that some board members want to plan day-to-day activities, which are strictly the responsibility of the executive. And second, some boards fail to establish a long-term plan, in which case the executive has no context in which to make short-term plans. How can they expect the executive to take the organization forward when they do not provide a written long-term plan? Without the long-term plan, the executive has to guess at what they want—and that can damage the relationship between board and executive.

8.   **Individual board members should attend board meetings and actively participate, including serving on committees and as officers.** How can the board conduct business when its members do not show up for meetings? Why do some board members fail to contribute anything? These are common questions asked by board members. When they volunteer to serve on the board, they should be active! If they cannot be active, they might want to reconsider their board membership. If they truly want to help the people served by the charity, they must know their proper role as a board member and be active in carrying out those responsibilities.

* * * * * * * * * *

218

The Benefits of Evaluation

General Job Description
Board of Directors
Anytown, Any Agency

Title: Member, Board of Directors

Purpose: To determine policies, procedures, and regulations for the governance of the organization; to raise the necessary funds to finance the organization and its programs; to evaluate the organization's effectiveness, and to evaluate the Executive Director (CEO).

Term: A maximum of six years with annual, biannual, or two three-year terms.

Meeting Attendance: The executive committee should have ten to twelve monthly meetings. The full board meets quarterly. Standing committees (vary as useful). Special events (as needed). Ad hoc committees (as needed).

Responsible to: The Chair of the Board is responsible to the Board of Directors. The Executive Director (CEO) to the Chair of the Board or other if designated.

Resignation of the Executive Director: In writing to the Chairman of the Board of Directors.

Responsibilities: The most important role of the board members is in the making of policies, long-range plans, and securing adequate funds for the continued operation of the organization.
- Selection, evaluation, and supervision of the executive director (CEO).
- Monitoring of expenditures within the organization's guidelines.
- Attending meetings regularly.

- Becoming well informed on all agenda items.
- Contributing knowledge and expressing points of view based on experience.
- Considering other points of view, making constructive suggestions, and helping the board make group decisions reflecting the thinking of the total group.
- Attending meetings of standing committees, as well as of any special ad hoc committees to which appointed.
- Personally giving financial support to the organization.
- Providing leadership in fund-raising efforts.
- Accepting leadership responsibilities as requested and when possible (such as committee chairperson or elected officer).
- Speaking on behalf of the organization when in attendance at community functions.
- Making an effort to become knowledgeable about the organization.
- Giving support to the director in times of crisis.

Standards of Performance for Staff and Volunteers

Standards of performance should be measured as frequently as needed. Some are measured annually, others quarterly. Very often it depends on the length of time the individual being measured has served in a particular capacity.

The senior development officer, often referred to as the executive director or CEO, should write all job descriptions for the staff and the volunteers. The executive does not necessarily need to have approval of the staff descriptions, but it would be prudent to have the board review any evaluation standard when volunteers might be held accountable.

The executive should write the descriptions in a form that can have measuring indicators so that measuring achievement against standards can take place.

Development Office Responsibilities

A five- or ten-year plan should be drafted for the charity by

The Benefits of Evaluation

the executive director. However, this is not the executive's responsibility. Even assuming that the executive has the expertise to write the first draft of the organization's long-range goals, the board is ultimately responsible for this task and should be thoroughly familiar with and give absolute approval of its content.

The annual plan is the sole responsibility of the executive director and should consider the appropriate allocation of staff, materials, and other resources applied to each piece of the plan.

The executive director also has the responsibility of developing the budget in such a way as to show cost of raising funds from each constituent base in each effort. The budget should be organized to allow for easy and useful monitoring plus comparison against the previous year.

Prospects and Donor Data

Is there an organization left on the face of this earth that doesn't realize the importance of keeping good records? Unfortunately, the answer is "yes," but I hope it's not anyone reading this book. Many kinds of computers and computer software are available today that will allow any development officer to keep good records. They vary in cost from a few hundred to many thousands of dollars. If you work in a new charity or a charity that is still rather small, you should start with an inexpensive system.

You must be able to keep an alpha list and the giving history for each donor. If you can get lists or reports from the software, so much the better. Reports can be helpful in prospecting and providing flat lists for volunteers to work from.

A flat list is a simple piece of paper with the alpha listing of some names you intend to work with.

The more advanced your computer software, the more extensive the profile development of selected, rated prospects you can have.

Useful Data

It will be helpful to you and your volunteers if you have

221

ready access to the number of new prospects that you identify monthly, quarterly, and annually. Where did these prospects come from? How many of the prospects were you able to convert to donors?

Once the prospects have become donors, you need to know how many contributed above a certain level and how many below. What zip code did they come from? Which volunteer workers had the best results?

Donor Records

You must have a <u>standardized</u> data record so that you can keep similar information on each prospect or donor. Names, addresses, pledges made, pledge payment, college attended, religious affiliation, hobbies, and so on. Be sure not to overlook in-kind gifts as part of the donors record. One of the greatest values of record keeping is that you can measure the upgrading of gifts and increasing involvement on the part of the donor.

Good Reports

A good report gives you a chronological gift history. Any donor who has been contributing for three or more years is an outstanding prospect to upgrade. In many cases, such a donor may have advanced to the point at which you feel that an approach for a planned gift is in order. How would you know this information without good records and good reports?

Remember that a donor's giving history is semi-confidential. Share this information with only those individuals who have a need to know. A misuse of this information can cause the board to question your judgment and a donor to cease supporting your charity.

Good records make it possible for you to evaluate the current year's revenue, volunteer involvement, and supply orders against last year's projections.

A monthly gift summary report arranged by sources (trustees, staff, foundations, corporations, etc.) and allocations and disbursements (unrestricted, scholarships, oncology department, etc.)

The Benefits of Evaluation

is a useful tool. This type of report could be widely distributed. However, if names are mentioned, confidentially becomes necessary.

Other useful reports include comparisons with the current month to the same period in previous years, of gift size, gift club and donor recognition levels, increasing gift levels, lapsed donors, first-time donors, and others.

The Fund-Raising Audit

Before we leave this chapter, it is important to talk briefly about the value and possible need for a fund-raising audit. A fund-raising audit isn't an audit of your books; it is intended to provide an objective review of a charity's internal development procedures. A fund-raising audit can be extremely helpful if your charity seems to have slipped into a rut and is routinely repeating the same projects year after year. The fund-raising or development audit is better conducted by professional fund-raising counsel. You need an objective view in which both you and your volunteer leadership have confidence.

Analyzing Data

At the end of each fund-raising year, gather information to be analyzed. The analysis provides the basis for a total program evaluation and for preparation of a new annual plan. Begin by evaluating the effectiveness of the staff involved in fund-raising projects. Review the job descriptions to determine if they are accurate against the goals you have set, and make sure that they consider the talent, training, and skill required for each job.

Review the plan of action and the actual achievements, and consider unscheduled or unforeseen changes. Review the plans of action, time lines, and results. Be sure that you have recorded the achievements and adjustments made during the year. Develop or correct new plans and new time lines. Analyze the budget, the chronological gift report, the summary gift report, and the performance of prospects and donors.

Fund Raising 101

Be sure that data from last years experience is organized according to categories—board, staff, doctors, and so on.

The data from this years fund rasing effort to be analyzed might include:

1. Number of gifts from each fund-raising category.
2. The total dollars raised in each category.
3. The average amount of each gift.

Compare these figures from the same data gathered from the previous year. (See Figure 34.)

Figure 34

	No. of gifts	Total $s Raised	Average Gift $	Last Yr Gifts	Last Yr $'s
from prospect mail	1,200	8,800	8	1123	8,130
direct mail	641	19,200	30	0	0
Corporate Gifts	3	15,000	5,000	3	15,000
Board/Trustees	24	6,725	280	23	6,445
Staff Gifts	9	3,675	408	9	3,675
Major Gifts	20	89,600	4,480	18	79,640
Walk-a-thon	600	3,234	5	532	2,665
County Walks	400	2,140	5	378	1,848
B/Tie/Auction	780	59,123	76	755	57,603
Memorials	160	4,000	25	160	4,000
Planned Gifts	3	20,000	6,666	3	20,000

Prospect Development:

Analyze your prospect development by answering the following questions:

1. What have you done to educate last years' prospects?
2. Was it adequate?
3. What will you do differently this year?
4. Were any new prospects added?
5. Is any work to be done on your list to clean it up, to make it a better, more usable list?

The Benefits of Evaluation

Reports that are necessary for making your analysis so that you can project next year's revenue are in the following categories, among others:

Trustees	Staff
Current donors	Prior donors
New donors	Corporations
Foundations	Associations
Government	

You need to know the cost data on each fund-raising project, so that you can determine the cost by programs:

Volunteer involvement: how many new volunteers were added, dropped, reassigned.

Communications activity: publications, news media, special events, and so on.

Support services: extent of staff support in gift receiving, posting, acknowledging, and thank-you letters.

Determine if the staffing was adequate and effective. Will you need in the future all the staff you currently have, or will you need more or less staff?

One of the most important evaluations concerns gift production results evaluated against goals. The following questions can help you make this determination:

1. Were dollar goals met within each category?
2. What contributed to success/failure?
3. What were this year's results compared with last year's gift income?
4. What number of cultivation or solicitation calls were made by the following:
   a. By the trustees?
   b. Chief executive?
   c. Development officers?
   d. Top-level volunteers?
   e. Other volunteers?

You will want this information for other categories such as annual gifts, major gifts, and for planned gifts.

1. Were each of the fund-raising methods that were selected used effectively?
   a. Personal calls?
   b. Personal letters?
   c. Direct mail?
   d. Gift clubs?
   e. Big gift solicitation?
   f. Planned gifts solicitation?
   g. Grants applications?
2. Which methods proved to be the most effective?
3. What increases or decreases were recorded in each category?
4. What were the number of planned gifts written and received during the year?
5. What was the number of planned gift cultivation solicitation calls made during the year?
6. How did expenditures compare with items in the development budget?
7. Was the budget, or categories within the budget, overspent and how can extra cost be justified?
8. What were the costs of fund raising by gifts in each of the fund-raising categories, and what was the ratio of costs to dollars produced overall?

Evaluation and Recommendations

Before you can create your next annual plan, determine if the information that you have gathered is adequate for evaluation against this past year's goals and objectives. Remember that any evaluation must include a measurement to determine if your projects and programs had adequate staff and volunteer support. If you met your financial goals but ran off your volunteers in the process, you need to know that and be prepared with a plan to counteract this in the future. Be sure that your action plans and time lines were accurate. If not, how should they be modified?

The Benefits of Evaluation

Don't overlook volunteer and staff assignments. Was the right person assigned to the right project. If not, what adjustments should be made? I am fortunate to have a wonderful staff. They make me look good everyday. One of the reasons they make me look good is that I observe their strengths and weaknesses and their likes and dislikes. I always try to assign the best person *for* each job *to* each job.

Our office has a wonderful woman who is responsible for data entry and keeping our donor records. I selected her because I felt that she possessed certain personality attributes for that position. In the interview, I looked for a person who paid meticulous attention to detail and who took pride in accuracy. I wanted her to be satisfied and happy even if she didn't talk with another person all day. With some luck, I was able to find the exact individual I was looking for. And, after working with her for a while, I began to notice other positive personality attributes that added to her value on our staff. She loved the minute details that are so much a part of the phon-a-thon. She went out of her way to have everything perfectly prepared and ready. She volunteered to work more nights than anyone else in the office. Because of these indicators, I gave her the phon-a-thon as her own project. Now, she is a bona fide fund raiser like the rest of us.

Confidence

Remember, *everyone*, staff and volunteers alike, will have more confidence in next year's plans if they are based on good research from last year's data.

Fund Raising 101

Chapter Nineteen

Total Quality Management

Together, we are about to solve the mystery of total quality management (TQM). I am of the opinion that most people who are good at fund raising are already practicing many of the total quality management techniques. I will not attempt to teach you all there is to know about TQM, but you are about to gain a better understanding of its purpose and use.

Let me demonstrate by asking two questions:
1. Do you delegate responsibility to volunteers and allow them to make decisions when they are confronted with the need to do so?

2. Do you thank and praise volunteers when they do something that helps your charity?

I'm guessing that you answered both questions positively. If I'm correct, you are already using two of the most important tenets in TQM. You empower people to make decisions, and you reward them when they deserve to be rewarded.

229

Total quality management is certainly more complicated than empowerment and praise, but if you do these two things, most of the rest falls into place.

A definition of total quality management might be *understanding who your customer is and making it as easy as possible for the customer to buy what they want, when they want, and at a price that makes the purchase a good value to them.*

In fund raising that translates into *understanding who your prospects are and making it as easy as possible for them to contribute what they want, when they want, and seeing that their donation achieves maximum value to those being served.*

If you were expecting total quality management to be more complicated, you must be disappointed. If I am not mistaken, I believe there is a verse from the Bible that could easily be used to explain TQM: "Do unto others as you wish them to do unto you.>>

By the way, TQM (total quality management) and QM (quality management) are interchangeable. They mean the same, and you are likely to see either or both used while reading or talking about quality.

Does Quality Management Work?

I should say so. An American, Dr. W. Edwards Deming, endeavored to get United States manufacturing companies to use the TQM method after World War II, but no one was interested at that time. American manufacturing was at its peak, and it appeared that nothing could change that. So Dr. Deming took the process to the Japanese, and they began using the methods right away. By the late 1950s, the Japanese were already beginning to compete successfully in the world market. By the 1980s they began to dominate. Currently, the Japanese supply:

*   More than 50 percent of the world's televisions
*   50 percent of the world's shipbuilding
*   70 percent of the world's microwaves
*   30 percent of the electronics in the United States
*   30 percent of the automobiles in the United States

Customers of Charities

To maximize the value of TQM, it is imperative that we identify who our customers are. Customers can vary, depending on the type of charity you are. However, all charities have some of the same customers, for example, volunteers, donors, and vendors. And you can subdivide each of these categories. Donors include foundations, corporations, local small businesses, wealthy individuals, not-so-wealthy individuals, and so on. You can subdivide volunteers and vendors also.

Quality Management Principles

Although you may see slightly different lists of TQM principles, they will always be similar to the following:

1.   Volunteer and donor satisfaction.

Volunteer and donor satisfaction translates into the happiness and satisfaction of your volunteers and donors with the work of your charity. Volunteers must be pleased with the method by which you relate to them and they to each other. They should take pride in being a volunteer for your charity.

Likewise, donors have to feel that they, too, are contributing and that their financial support is appreciated and used appropriately.

2.   Respect for your volunteers, donors, and clients (Clients being the recipients of your charity's fund raising).

This principle is intended to help your charity to maintain or improve its performance regarding the clients while meeting the needs of the volunteers and donors. With continuous improvement, the volunteers and donors become better satisfied with your services.

3.   Continual improvement is necessary.

All your volunteers, staff, and donors are continually working to improve the projects and programs that your charity conducts, so that they add long-term value from the perspective of the charity's volunteers and donors.

4.   Processes and prevention.

If your charity stresses the prevention of mistakes by the continuous planning and evaluation of its projects and programs, those processes will automatically improve.

5.   Manage your charity by using facts and data.

A charity should base its decisions on the facts and data concerning a particular decision. For example, if you conducted a special event last year that used 972 volunteer hours, 96 staff man hours, cost $2,500 and raised only $1,230, you probably will not want to conduct that particular project again. However, you wouldn't necessarily know that if you didn't keep good records.

6.   All managers and leaders must lead.

The mission and vision statements must come from the leaders of the organization. And they, too, must be visible in support of the mission and vision statements.

D. Scott Sink, another TQM guru, says, "*You'll know you've succeeded when you're out-performing your competitors and you don't have a name for your program; it's just the way you do business.*"

A Way of Life

Many of the current leaders in total quality management worry that charities will accept TQM as just another management philosophy, use it for a while, and then discard it as they have done with other past management styles. For TQM to work, it has to become a part of your organization, a part of your everyday life. If it is merely a program, it will become passé and soon disappear.

One of Deming's more important philosophies is that people aren't usually the cause of the problem; it's most often the system. That's one philosophy that I can agree with. A local Kingsport, Tennessee, attorney, Shelburne Ferguson, Jr, who writes a weekly column for our newspaper on business and charities, recently used the following example of the United States legislature. He said, "Let's take Congress for example. The cry is to clean House . . . and Senate. While a clean sweep might slow down some of the bone-headed things Washington politicians do, placing a new bunch of politicians in the same system isn't likely to change much. Think about it. Over the last 25 years, just about every member of Congress has changed anyway. Some died; some chose not to run;

others were defeated. Yet nothing much has changed. Scandals continue. Selfishness rules. It's business as usual. So if we get the same result, no matter who works in the system, which is the culprit—the individual or the system?"

It's been my experience that people want to be successful; they want to do the job right. Admittedly, there are some people who are lazy or want something for nothing, but they are in the minority. Give most people the chance to work and contribute and feel the dignity that comes with self-reliance, and they will make any supervisor proud of them.

We all strive to reach our charity's goals and objectives, and we want to be considerate of our volunteers and donors. I'm sure you work as hard as I do to accomplish those objectives. Total quality management can help us all. By simply becoming interested in the process, we will learn more about how to organize and plan and how to focus on the needs of all the volunteers and donors we serve. We will learn better techniques for teamwork and evaluation.

How Does Quality Management Work?
It is a five-step process:
1. Suppliers
2. Input
3. Processes
4. Outputs
5. Customers

In a special event for an art museum, for example, those five steps translate into:
1. Volunteers and donors
2. Dollars given to charity
3. Art work purchased or created
4. Art work viewed and enjoyed
5. Public satisfaction

Management Styles
When I entered the work force in the late 1950s, most of my

bosses were tough and gave the impression that they knew everything there was to know about the job. Today, all managers of charities face spiraling costs, increasing competition, the need for stronger ethics, changes in industry, and donors who demand to know how their money is spent. The 1990s are not going to be noted as a time when managers of charities had it easy. The old management styles are not as effective as they were in times past. As fund-raising volunteers or executives, we must change or we won't be able to keep pace.

I began my employment as a fund raiser with a national philanthropy in the early 1970s. On a long drive one day, my supervisor began talking about the good ole days. "All you needed was a store front with the window taken out. People would drive by and toss money through the window," he said. He was referring to the time immediately after Doctor Jonas Salk developed the vaccine to prevent polio.

We all realize this wasn't literally true, but he was saying that fund raising for the March of Dimes was not too difficult for a while back then. Those days no longer exist for the March of Dimes or for any other charity.

If the managers of charities are to be effective in today's climate, they must be better than the next charity at managing and challenging their volunteers. They will have to be able to recruit, train, motivate, and most important, delegate responsibility to them. It is important that we recognize these facts as truths and also realize that it is we, you and I, to whom I am referring.

Recommended Reading

Recommended Reading and Viewing

American Fund Raising Institute® - Videos. *How You Ask Makes The Difference.* Kingsport, TN - 1992

Ashton, Debra. *The Complete Guide to Planned Giving: Everything You Need to Know to Compete Successfully for Major Gifts.* Cambridge, MA: JLA Publications, 1988.

Balthauser, William F. *Call for Help: How to Raise Philanthropic Funds with Phonathons.* Ambler, PA: The Fund Raising Institute, 1983.

Berendt, Robert, and J. Richard Taft. *How to Rate Your Development Department.* Washington, DC: The Taft Group, 1984.

Burlingame, Dwight F., and Lamont J. Hulse. *Taking Fund Raising Seriously: Advancing the Profession and Practice of Raising Money.* San Francisco, CA: Jossey-Bass Publishers, 1991.

Dannelley, Paul. *Fund Raising and Public Relations: A Critical Guide to Literature and Resources.* Norman, OK: University of Oklahoma Press, 1986.

Dove, Kent. *Conducting a Successful Capital Campaign: A Comprehensive Fundraising Guide for Nonprofit Organizations.* San Francisco, CA: Jossey-Bass Publishers, Inc., 1988.

Gurin, Maurice G. *Confessions of a Fund Raiser: Lessons of an Instructive Career.* Washington, DC: The Taft Group, 1985.

Hardy, James M. *Managing for Impact in Nonprofit Organizations: Corporate Planning Techniques and Applications.* Erwin, TN: Essex Press, 1984.

Huntsinger, Jerald E. *Fund Raising Letters: A Comprehensive Study Guide to Raising Money by Direct Mail Response Marketing.* Richmond, VA: Emerson Publishers, 1985.

Jenkins, Jeanne B., and Marilyn Lucas. *How to Find Philanthropic Prospects.* Ambler, PA: The Fund Raising Institute, 1986.

Kiritz, Norton J. *Program Planning and Proposal Writing.* Los Angeles, CA: The Grantsmanship Center, 1980.

Knott, Ronald A. *The Makings of a Philanthropic Fundraiser: The Instructive Example of Milton Murray.* San Francisco, CA: Jossey-Bass Publishers, Inc., 1992.

Lord, James Gregory. *Philanthropy and Marketing.* Cleveland, OH: Third Sector Press, 1982.

Seymour, Harold J. *Designs for Fund Raising: Principles, Patterns, Techniques.* New York: McGraw-Hill, 1966.

Sharpe, Robert F. *Before You Give Another Dime.* Nashville, TN: Thomas Nelson Publishers, 1979.

Recommended Advanced Reading

* * * * * * * * * * * * * * * * * * *

Greenfield, James M. *Fund-Raising: Evaluating and Managing the Fund Development Process.* New York, NY: John Wiley & Sons, Inc., 1991.

Rosso, Henry A. *Achieving Excellence in Fund Raising: A Comprehensive Guide to Principles, Strategies, and Methods.* San Francisco, CA: Jossey - Bass Publishers, 1991.